January 30th /04.

Elizabeth!

A little bit of Canadian propaganda
to express our appreciation for what
you are doing for the college and
particularly making me look good
during my presidential year!
We look forward to seeing more
of you. The college is in your
debt. Many thanks

Sincerely

P.S. Look for
Y.O.B.S. on pg. 13.

CANADA
A PORTRAIT

(Previous page)
Girl from Bathurst Inlet,
Northwest Territories.
Photo by
Richard Harrington,
CMCP.

Sled dog puppies,
Nunavut.
Photo by Mike Beedell.

(This page)
Yum Yum Bus,
Nova Scotia.
Photo by John Sylvester.

© Minister of Industry, 2002

Available in Canada through authorized
bookstore agents and other bookstores or from:

Statistics Canada
Circulation Management
Dissemination Division
120 Parkdale Avenue
Ottawa, Ontario
K1A 0T6
Toll-free Order Line: 1 800 267-6677
Fax: 1 877 287-4369
E-mail: order@statcan.ca

The National Library of Canada has catalogued
this publication as follows:

Main entry under title:

Canada: a portrait

57th ed.
Issued also in French under title:
Un portrait du Canada.

Catalogue no. 11-403-XPE
ISBN 0-660-18826-0

1. Canada — Economic conditions —
Periodicals.
2. Canada — Social conditions — Periodicals.
3. Canada — Politics and government —
Periodicals.
4. Canada — Description and travel —
Periodicals.

La présente publication est également
disponible en français.

Design: Neville Smith, Aviva Furman
Composition: Suzanne Beauchamp, Louise Demers

Printed by Imprimerie Transcontinental Inc.
Beauceville Est, Quebec.

Printed in Canada

The 57th edition
of Canada: A
Portrait, published
under the authority
of the Minister of
Industry.

FOREWORD

I am pleased to present this *57*th edition of *Canada: A Portrait* and I am honoured to thank the eminent thinkers, poets, writers, and actors who have joined with us in presenting a very human and evocative look at the Canada of the new millennium.

We are especially indebted to John Kenneth Galbraith, Gordon Pinsent, Guy Vanderhaeghe, Rick Mercer, Nicole Brossard and Zacharias Kunuk, all of whom have written of their personal connections to this great and wonderful land of ours.

Together with their insights and drawing on the statistical work of our Agency, we have sought to present a clear and dynamic view of the social, economic and cultural lives of our citizenry. To complete this portrait, we have drawn also on the stories and memories of our nation to give context and meaning to the experiences of the day.

I join with my colleagues here at Statistics Canada in extending to all our readers our hope that they will find this edition of *Canada: A Portrait* both relevant and useful to a greater understanding of the Canada of today and of the future ahead.

Ivan P. Fellegi

Chief Statistician of Canada

ACKNOWLEDGEMENTS

On behalf of Statistics Canada, I am honoured to acknowledge and thank the *Portrait* team. I am above all grateful to Penny Stuart for her extraordinary contribution to this project. As Production Manager and Senior English Editor, Penny brought together a unique blend of timing, analytical thinking, and plain old-fashioned fun to what might otherwise have been a fairly arduous undertaking. Together with Penny, I wish also to thank the team who all helped to create this book.

We thank especially our editorial team: chapter writers Phil Jenkins ("The Land"), Gordon Priest ("The People"), Helen Smith ("The Society"), Ken Ross ("Arts and Leisure"), Van Whitehead ("The Economy"), and Gareth Spanglett ("Canada in the World"), as well as feature writers Sandra Nicholls, Randy Ray and our writer-at-large Bruce Nesbitt. A special thanks to Patricia Buchanan and Monique Dumont for the English and French indexes and to Claire Quintal and Joyce Thomas for editorial help. Many thanks also to Janis Camelon, head of English writing and editing, and her team: Elizabeth Irving, Helen Kampf, Tim Prichard, Robin Redmond, Yan Thériault and Nick Thorp for incisive and thorough editorial help.

A special note of appreciation also must go to Ginette Lavoie, Senior French Editor and Co-ordinator for her patience and great skill, as well as to editors Judith Côté, Christine Duchesne, Marie-Paule Robert, Nathalie Villemure and Louis Majeau for their commitment to this project, and, for guidance, Annie Lebeau, head of French writing and editing. We are indebted to the Official Languages Division and Translation services for their help to us, as well as to François Bordé, our Assistant Director.

Our editorial team is supported and sustained through a network of analysts working both within and outside Statistics Canada. Many thanks to Mary Cromie, Gordon Dekker, David Dodds, Michel Durand, John Gordon, Hugh Henderson, Steven Mozes, Scott Murray, Doug Norris, Willa Rea, Paul Reed, Art Ridgeway, Philip Ryan, Ray Ryan, Mehrzad Salem, George Sciadas, Wayne Smith, Maryanne Webber, Carolyn Weiss, Karen Wilson and Michael Wolfson. A special note of appreciation must go, as always, to the staff of Statistics Canada's Library, and also to Professor John Warkentin of York University for his astute and much-appreciated guidance on "The Land."

We are grateful also to Jacques Lefebvre and his group of analysts—Monique Beyrouti, Isabel Dias, François Lavoie, Andrew Mackenzie, Jacqueline Tebbens and Kelly Tran—all of whom matched pen with wit and statistical savvy to help us create text that is readable and informative.

For harmonizing creative concerns with the business case, our appreciation goes out to the CAP steering committee. Special thanks to Louis Boucher, Vicki Crompton, Iain McKellar, David Roy and Martin Podehl. Special appreciation also to Johanne Beauseigle, Chief, Design and Production Services, for business acumen and technical management and to Louise Demers and Suzanne Beauchamp for their hard work and excellence in the art of composition and their commitment to this project. Our thanks and appreciation to Francine Pilon-Renaud for shepherding the *Portrait* through the printing world.

Producing the *Portrait* is half the challenge; marketing and selling it the other. In this endeavour, we are lucky to have the involvement of Marc Bazinet and Gabrielle Beaudoin and, for his success on the sales front, we acclaim John Whitton.

I am, as always, honoured to have worked with Neville Smith and Aviva Furman, whose designs bring support, conviction and power to the themes of the *Portrait*. To Susan Bernard, for her work as our photo editor, we extend our gratitude for the depth and intelligence of her research.

Finally, I wish to offer a word of thanks to Emily Burton, for her assiduous work as researcher, Monique Poirier, production co-ordinator, for grace under pressure; and to Vicki Crompton, new to Communications Division as Director, but a kind and gracious supporter withal.

Jonina Wood

Editor-in-Chief, *Canada: A Portrait*

TABLE OF CONTENTS

Red maple sapling.
Photo by
J. David Andrews.

From the time I was a very young child growing up in

Grand Falls, Newfoundland, I remember this huge rock

that was out overlooking the cove. I spent a lot of time on

that rock, and I remember it was always warm, even in bad

weather. A large, warm, smooth rock.

In a way, I feel this land is my partner and no matter where

I go in the world, I can draw on my partnership to this

country and to that rock on the cove and I find solace and

inspiration.

Gordon Pinsent, actor

Lake Superior.

Photo by

Hélène Anne Fortin.

THE LAND

"As I begin to tell this, it is the golden month of September in southwestern Ontario. In the splendid autumn sunshine the bounty of the land is almost overwhelming as if it is the manifestation of a poem by Keats."

In these opening lines from his fine novel *No Great Mischief*, the Canadian writer Alistair MacLeod illuminates the splendour of a Canadian season and the richness of the Ontario countryside. MacLeod, who hails from Cape Breton, believes "you carry a landscape within you" and the truth of his ringing statement is at the heart of Canada's story. That story begins with the land, and within every Canadian, new or old, is an appreciation of it, based on their experience of this tough, glorious, vast northern landscape.

Alistair MacLeod is just one of a long line of writers who have articulated their experience of Canada, the look of it and the rhythm of its seasons—seasons that change like sets in a history play.

"Wait a while; you know nothing of a Canadian winter," a neighbour told Susanna Moodie in 1832, shortly after she had immigrated to Upper Canada, as Ontario was then known. "This is only November; after the Christmas thaw, you'll know something about cold." Moodie came to know the winters well, and wrote of them in a book whose title could be a bumper sticker for early Canadian immigrant history, *Roughing it in the Bush*.

Almost two centuries and one season later, Sharon Butala of southern Saskatchewan wrote, in *The Perfection of the Morning*: "On a warm spring day riding a horse, walking or travelling in a truck across true shortgrass prairie that had never known a plow in all its history since the glaciers, I thought I had never smelled anything so wonderful in all my life…" After the prelude of spring comes the season when, according to Nova Scotian poet George Elliott Clarke, the fields are "maddened, by chlorophyll" and we can "stray outside, bumble around a geyser of raspberries that erupts crooked from black soil."

The story of Canada also includes the tale of a young nation built on the solid foundation of an old land. Near Hebron Fiord in Labrador there are rocks, among the most ancient in Canada, that testify to a massive shield of igneous and metamorphic rock, the bedrock of half of Canada, formed more than three and a half billion years ago, in the time before seasons. A billion years later, Canada's first life appeared— simple organisms that left their trace in the oldest fossils discovered so far at Steep Rock Lake, near Atikokan, in Ontario.

Much later in the geographical story of Canada—a mere million years ago—the great ice sheets advanced south a number of times. The Keewatin and Labrador sheets reached past our southern border as far as Wisconsin and New York State, then melted away. Even before the ice age ended, one theory has it, nomads migrated over a now-sunken land bridge from Asia to the Aleutian Islands, moving south down a corridor between ice lobes, then spreading eastward, then north into the warming land—the geographical expanse that would become Canada.

The story of Canadian geography is written on a page that takes up 9,984,670 square kilometres, making Canada the second largest country in the world. The length of continuous highway—the Trans-Canada—needed to traverse this tremendous space is 7,821 kilometres. The longest national highway in the world, it took 20 years to build—from 1950 to 1970.

A driver setting out from 'point zero' of the Trans-Canada in St. John's, Newfoundland, and heading all the way to Victoria, British Columbia, would have to reset the car clock five times while crossing six time zones. Anyone wishing to leave the car at home and take the walk of a lifetime could set out on the Trans Canada Trail. Begun as part of Canada's 125th birthday celebrations in 1992, it is almost twice as long as the Trans-Canada Highway.

The great bulk of the Canadian mainland is bookended by Vancouver Island in the west and Newfoundland in the east, while a collection of islands in the Canadian

"There's a whisper

on the night-wind,

there's a star agleam

to guide us,

And the wild is

calling, calling...

let us go."

Robert Service,
Songs of a Sourdough, 1907

Quiet moment near
Kamouraska, Quebec.
Photo by Éric Piché,
ALT-6.

Archipelago crown the northern sea. The world's largest group of islands includes Axel Heiberg, Ellesmere and Baffin Island, Canada's largest island, which is home to, among others, the white Peary caribou, millions of thick-billed murres and 11,340 people.

At its widest, Canada stretches 5,500 kilometres, from the eastern tip of Newfound-land, the first piece of land the rising sun strikes in North America, to the beginning of the Yukon–Alaska border. From Canada's southernmost point in Lake Erie to the most northerly on Ellesmere Island is a distance of 4,600 kilometres.

Three oceans—the Atlantic, Pacific and Arctic—absorb the outflow of dozens of rivers along Canada's crenulated mainland coastline, 58,059 kilometres long. Adding in the perimeters of our legions of islands stretches it to 243,792 kilometres, making it the longest national coastline in the world, six times the Earth's circumference. Beyond the coast, the land slips under water to form a continental shelf, the true unseen edge of the continent.

The Story Unfolds

This massive accretion of land, the north of North America, is a jigsaw of ecozones, 15 in all, each with its own 'personality traits' of climate, topography and wildlife. There are muskox herds in the North Arctic ecozone and vines in the Mixedwood Plains of southern Ontario. Wolverines roam the Taiga Cordillera in the extreme northwest. On the Hudson Plain on the southern rim of the inland sea that is Hudson Bay, there are dwarf birch trees and aspen.

In Canada's Pacific Maritime ecozone, giant forests are home to cougars and grizzly bears, and salmon make their run to and from the sea. Beyond the north–south rampart of the Rocky Mountains and the Montane Cordillera, the central grasslands run on like a rumpled quilt below wide open sky. The Prairie and Boreal Plains ecozones yield to the woodlands of the Boreal Shield again, more deciduous than in the west.

At the interface of prairie and woodland, in the Hudson Plain and scattered in many parts of Canada, lie the 1.3 million square kilometres of richly inhabited wetlands, providing a nesting place for the swamp sparrow and a stomping ground for the moose. Wetlands make up an eighth of the total land area of Canada. In the Atlantic Maritime ecozone, the woodlands march on to the rugged ocean coast.

To the north, beyond the tree line—the dividing zone between boreal forest and tundra—the broad-shouldered Arctic remains white in the northern cryosphere (the collective term for ice and snow deposits). In this land, day and night are measured not with a clock but with a calendar, and, at the higher elevations (such as Ellesmere and Baffin), the ice age never ended.

The story of Canadian settlement continues with a wave of migrants who came across the Atlantic Ocean from Europe and set their roots in the land, harvesting the coastal fisheries, the fur-bearing wildlife, the far-reaching forests, and the minerals and metals below. A country emerged from this alloy of European immigrants and a host of Aboriginal tribes. The country became Canada from *Kanata*, a St. Lawrence Iroquois word that Jacques Cartier heard while he was sailing upriver in 1535. Later, it was named the Dominion of Canada at Confederation in 1867.

As the story unfolded, new lines were drawn as the shape of the political boundaries emerged. In 1906, the first national atlas of Canada was produced, the year after Saskatchewan and Alberta entered Confederation. The modern map of Canada shows 10 provinces and three territories that together make up the Canadian federation.

The population spread out across this map has now surpassed 30 million. This means that if we were to space ourselves evenly over the country, there would be approximately 3.3 people to each square kilometre of land. Compare that with the United States, where there are about 30.7 people per square kilometre, or with Russia, where there are 8.5.

"Long warped fingers held up, trembling before an old face like a stone on the prairie, the noise of ten thousand buffalo cupped in his broken hands."

Margaret Sweatman,
*When Alice Lay Down
With Peter, 2001*

Somewhere in Nunavut.
Photo by Mike Beedell.

The vast majority of Canadians live within 200 kilometres of the United States–Canada border, in a cross-country belt of urban centres with Winnipeg as the buckle. Of the 27 most populated cities, 19 lie within this band and house 57% of the population. Viewed over time, the Canadian story is one of a population forsaking the section for the city street.

In 1901, with the population of Canada at 5.4 million, some 40% of Canadians were directly involved in agriculture. By 1999, the number of farmers had dwindled to less than 3% of the population. Canadian farms, although 18.3% fewer in number than in 1976, are now on average 22% larger. In fact, many family farms have given way to huge corporate farming enterprises.

The North

In 1925, a six-man expedition sailed up the Pacific coast, disembarked and struck out for the massive St. Elias Mountains. After a trek lasting 65 gruelling days, the men conquered Canada's highest peak, Mount Logan, named in 1890 after Sir William Logan, first head of the Geological Survey of Canada. Mount Logan is just a few metres short of 6,000, and 10 times taller than the loftiest piece of human engineering in Canada, the CN Tower in Toronto. It is the second highest peak in North America, second only to Alaska's Mount McKinley, although it doesn't register on a list of the world's 100 tallest mountains.

From the summit of Mount Logan, climbers have an unprecedented view east toward the Yukon, the Northwest Territories and Nunavut. Together, these three territories constitute about 40% of Canada's land mass, a Nordic area the size of Europe, and are home to 92,800 people. Canada's most northerly named point, Cape Columbia on Ellesmere Island, lies just past 83 degrees north latitude, 720 kilometres shy of the North Pole. In the coldest months, the trek across the ice from Ellesmere to Canada's close neighbour, Greenland, is a mere 26 kilometres at the shortest distance.

The Ghost.
Princess Royal Island,
British Columbia.
Photo by Ron Thiele.

The Ghost Bears Along the northwest coast of British Columbia, there lives a small population of white Kermode bears, also known as the ghost or spirit bears. While their numbers are cloaked in mystery—they live far from people—it's estimated they number about 100 to 200 and are nowhere to be found on the planet except here, in the rainforests of Canada's West Coast.

According to a Tsimshian First Nations legend, Raven came down long ago from the heavens and went among the black bears turning every 10th one white—the colour of glaciers.

The Tsimshians call this unique bear Moksgm'ol, or simply white bear. More popularly, it's known as the Kermode, after Francis Kermode, a curator of the British Columbia Provincial Museum who studied these creatures in the early 1900s. Recent findings show that the bears' white colouring is caused by a single mutation in the DNA sequence of their coat colour gene. Since this mutation is recessive, it is possible for two black bears to produce a white cub.

In 2001, some 1,350 square kilometres from Princess Royal Island and adjacent lands were set aside as a natural reserve for all time. A good beginning, say the bears' protectors, but still just a beginning. Many more thousands of hectares must be set aside to ensure the survival of the ghost bear… not to mention the vision of Raven.

Fifty thousand Inuit live in the North: the Inuvialuit, Copper Inuit and Netsilik peoples. Northern Canada has a population density of 0.03 people per square kilometre, a mere one-hundredth of the national distribution. The population is concentrated in the three territorial capitals: Whitehorse, where 21,400 people and two out of three Yukoners live; Yellowknife, Northwest Territories, with 16,600 people and two gold mines within the city limits; and Nunavut's Iqaluit, which means 'place of fish' in Inuktitut and has a population of 5,200.

The North, because its vegetation is so slow to grow, displays its history of habitation like an open book. Tent rings and the ash of fireplaces long gone cold reveal occupation going back over 12,000 years to the Athapaskan people, who were followed by the Inuit 8,000 years later. On Kodlunarn Island in Countess of Warwick Sound, the ruins of the abandoned minings of Englishman Martin Frobisher in 1578 testify to the arrival of the Europeans much later.

Many of the Arctic explorers were in search of the Northwest Passage, the imagined waterway that would take explorers and traders between the Atlantic and Pacific. Though most tried to sail through, one man—Samuel Hearne—attempted to locate it on foot and recorded his troubled travels in the remarkable document *A Journey from Prince of Wales's Fort in Hudson's Bay to the Northern Ocean undertaken by order of the Hudson's Bay Company for the Discovery of Copper Mines, a North-West Passage, &c. in the Years 1769, 1770, 1771, & 1772*. Hearne, led by Matonabbee, a famous Chipewyan guide, made a trek worthy of an adventure movie but did not find the passage. It was not until 1905 that the Norwegian explorer Roald Amundsen, after a three-year sojourn west to east in the *Gjoa*, broke out into the Beaufort Sea and proved the ocean-to-ocean journey possible.

By the Pacific

When the explorer Alexander Mackenzie reached the Pacific in 1793, he noted that the waters before him were "much inter spers'd with Island." Mackenzie was unaware that the land before him lay in an area of relative geological unrest. Canadian geology is a story still in motion, nowhere more so than along the Pacific coast. In 1700, one of the world's largest recorded earthquakes, scored later as 9 out of a possible 10 on the Richter scale, collapsed many homes of the Cowichan people on Vancouver Island. In 2001, some 26 earthquakes shook the region, one of which knocked objects from shelves in the Queen Charlotte Islands.

British Columbia is a medley of landscapes and climatic zones. The largest single-day snowfall in Canadian history—enough to bury a standing person—fell at Lake Tahtsa near Kitimat in February, 1999. On the other hand, the semi-arid southern interior of the province is the country's dry spot, home to scorpions and rattlesnakes. The highest yearly average temperature, the longest annual average frost-free period, and the lowest annual average snowfall in Canada were all recorded in southwestern British Columbia. By contrast, in the northern part of the province, the average January temperature is −20°C.

Just over half of British Columbia's 3.9 million inhabitants live in the mountain-ringed city of Vancouver. Overall, the province has a population density of 4.2 people per square kilometre.

In terms of agriculture, there is ranching in the heartland, apple orchards and vine-yards in the Okanagan Valley, and floriculture and berry crops along the mild, moist coast. In the northeast, where conditions are similar to the Prairies, grains and oilseeds are the staple crops.

The Prairies

Canada's Prairie provinces sit neatly on North America's 49th parallel, which was mapped out by a joint Boundary Commission beginning in 1872 and was marked by a series of mounds set at 4.8-kilometre intervals. Where the boundary passes through bush or forest, a six-metre wide path called a 'vista' now shows where the United States ends and Canada begins. The entire frontier between Canada and the United States, the longest shared border in the world, extends for 8,891 kilometres.

"I swam in two oceans this summer, played golf in four provinces, went horse racing in three others, and was bitten by bugs in nearly all."

Peter Gzowski, *The New Morningside Papers*, 1987

Allan's Corner, Quebec.

Photo by Jean Bruneau,

ALT-6.

Tabletop-flat for the most part, the Prairies are covered in a deep fertile clay soil left by glaciers and glacial lakes. In explorer David Thompson's day, as many as 70 million plains bison ranged across these grasslands. Eventually, the plains bison were hunted to near extinction. Today, some survive on commercial farms and in small wild herds, such as the 600 bison roaming within Elk Island National Park near Edmonton. Some 5.1 million people live in the Prairie provinces, half of them in Calgary, Edmonton and Winnipeg. In terms of population density, Alberta's is most concentrated at 4.6 people per square kilometre and Saskatchewan's, the least at a mere 1.7.

The western edge of Alberta is a kilometre higher than the boundary of eastern Manitoba, known as the keystone province because of its central position in the provincial line-up. Water thus makes a downhill journey through the region by the Assiniboine and Saskatchewan rivers to the Red River and Lake Winnipeg and on toward Hudson Bay.

By one of those quirks of immigration that make Canadian history so interesting, it is possible to buy a newspaper from Iceland in several towns in the Interlake region of Manitoba. The region was homesteaded by Icelanders fleeing their country, which was racked by disasters such as erupting volcanoes. In 1875, a group of 235 recently immigrated Icelanders left Winnipeg in flatboats, travelled to the shore of Lake Winnipeg and there founded New Iceland, a settlement centred around Gimli. The cultural tie thrives to this day.

In the southern Prairies, the land is pockmarked with sloughs, varying in size from large puddles to lakes. In the spring, meltwater and rain transform the region from a blanket of white into a straw bed studded with mirror-like, freshwater wetlands. Nearly two-fifths of Canada's wetlands—areas of land underwater for at least part of the day or year—lie in the Alberta, Saskatchewan, Manitoba triumvirate. Since European settlement, it is estimated that 71% of the wetlands in the Prairie provinces have been converted to agricultural use, a loss of habitat for many species, from protozoans and aquatic insects to waterfowl and mammals.

Castor canadensis In 1931, the great conservationist Grey Owl ranked the beaver with the maple leaf as a fitting representative of the Dominion: "This little worker of the wild," he wrote, "has been much honoured. He...has [truly] won a place as one of Canada's national emblems, by the example he gives of industry, adaptability, and dogged perseverance…"

Perhaps no animal has influenced a country's history as much as the beaver has influenced that of Canada. It began with a passion for fur that took Europe by storm in the late 16th century. The European fur market became in turn a key impetus for exploration and even settlement of Canada, drawing explorers—Champlain, Radisson and Des Groseilliers, to name just a few—deep into the Canadian wilderness in pursuit of beaver pelts.

In fact, the beaver was the axis upon which Canada's early economy turned and at its peak, fur traders were able to sell some 200,000 beaver pelts a year to the European market, most of them to be made into hats. By the mid-1800s, silk had replaced beaver as the hat fabric of choice, in part because trapping had seriously depleted the beaver population.

Grey Owl was so taken with the beaver and so admired its intelligence that he adopted several from the Canadian wilds—McGinty

and McGinnis, Jelly Roll and Rawhide—and wrote about them. In the 1930s, he led the struggle to help preserve Canada's beavers and, through his efforts, a movement to save them began. Eventually trapping laws were changed and populations once again grew.

The beaver is an impressive architect, one of the few mammals other than humans able to manufacture its own environment. Beavers build dams and construct canals. Some of their dams can be as high as 5.5 metres, and their lodges are so sophisticated they could come complete with architectural drawings.

The beaver has made many emblematic appearances: it is featured on the coats of arms of the Hudson's Bay Company and the City of Montréal, the crest of the Canadian Pacific Railway company, the first postage stamp (the Three Penny 'Beaver'), and the reverse side of the nickel. An "act to provide for the recognition of the beaver (*Castor canadensis*) as a symbol of the sovereignty of Canada" received royal assent in 1975.

Today, about one thousand place names in Canada—Beaver Crossing, Alberta, Lac Castor Blanc, Quebec, and Beaver River, Nova Scotia, to name just three—are named for the beaver. It also makes a proud appearance on the cover of this edition of *Canada: A Portrait* in the form of an illustration by Neville Smith.

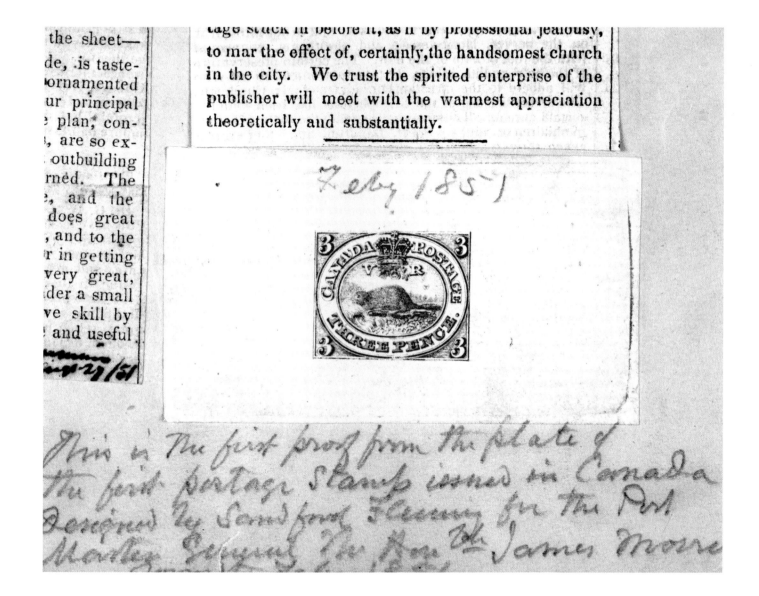

Three Penny 'Beaver,' 1851.

National Archives of Canada,

Acc. 1989-565.

In the summer of 1857, Irishman John Palliser led an expedition into the Prairies, concluding that here was a vast, latent grassland, much of it suitable for agriculture with a southern semi-arid zone now called Palliser's Triangle. Palliser's bounteous prediction has come true; all but a fifth of Canada's arable farmland lies in this region, and the annual crop from the fields of wheat, oats, barley, rye, canola and flaxseed is enough to provide every one of Canada's 30 million people with over one tonne of food. As farmers there know, the land is susceptible to droughts and punishing winds—one hot spell in southern Saskatchewan pushed the mercury up to 45°C on July 15, 1937, the highest temperature so far recorded in Canada.

Canada Central

When French sailor Jacques Cartier named the small bay he anchored in on August 10, 1535 after the relevant saint, St. Lawrence, he had no idea that this appellation would spread to encompass an entire river. Author Frances Brooke, the wife of an army chaplain posted to Quebec, later described it as "one of the noblest in the world" in the very first Canadian novel, *The History of Emily Montague*, written in 1769. The river was to eventually ferry millions of Europeans, like Brooke and her husband, into the heartland of Canada.

The St. Lawrence is the longest east–west river on the continent and, in its lower reaches, is the natural habitat of nine species of whale, including the leviathan blue whale. The adjacent central provinces of Ontario and Quebec together add up to 2,282,869 square kilometres, one-quarter of Canada's total land mass. Three-fifths of Canada's citizens—18.6 million people—now live in these provinces. One-quarter of the national populace lives in the two biggest cities: Toronto and Montréal, home to 4.7 million and 3.4 million inhabitants, respectively. Ontario, with 12.4 people per square kilometre, has more than twice the population density of Quebec, at 5.3.

The central provinces display a varied landscape, dominated in the north by the Canadian Shield: a mosaic of forests, rocky outcrops, lakes and rivers. Ancient hills attract skiers in the winter and numerous lakes draw cottagers in the summer. Lowlands and flood plains flank mighty rivers like the Ottawa, the St. Maurice and the Richelieu, and great swaths of mixed forest coat the hills, with the coniferous trees holding fast to the green in the fall as the deciduous trees turn from green to yellow, orange and red.

The towering timber stands of white pine along the St. Lawrence were used for the shipbuilding industry as early as 1665, under the first Intendant of New France, Jean Talon. Lumbering has thrived in the eastern woodlands ever since, helped by the region's rapids and waterfalls that can power the saws and lumber mills. At the end of the 19th century, the biggest sawmills in the world clustered around the Chaudière Falls in Ottawa.

The noise of trees falling continues in the forest. Quebec, Canada's largest province and host to the largest stand of forest south of the 60th parallel, produces two-fifths of the country's paper. The tree harvest is moving into new territory and new controversy. The Northern Boreal Initiative, an Ontario government project, will open up several million hectares of slow-growing trees such as black spruce for the forestry industry.

Numerous islands are found in the St. Lawrence and the Great Lakes. Rugged, boggy Anticosti Island, situated at the mouth of the St. Lawrence, is home to 300 people and 100,000 white-tailed deer and is larger than Prince Edward Island by more than 2,000 square kilometres. Farther west, just downstream from Québec, lies Grosse Île, which served as Canada's quarantine station from 1832 to 1937 and was the first piece of Canada upon which many immigrants set foot. Then, above the Lachine Rapids lie the islands that form the heart of Montréal, a city that is home to over one-tenth of the Canadian population.

"...the autumn, achingly beautiful, the Laurentian hills ablaze with colour, the skies a deep hard blue."

Mordecai Richler,
Home Sweet Home, 1984

25

In Ontario, the timelessly beautiful Thousand Islands (shared with New York State) lie in the St. Lawrence River at the eastern edge of Lake Ontario. There are actually 1,149 in all. The Thirty Thousand Islands, a second group of islands distinguished by the label 'thousand,' festoon Georgian Bay. On the north side lies Manitoulin, the largest inland island in the world.

By the Atlantic

"...a massive assertion of land, sea's end, the outer limit of all the water in the world, a great, looming sky-obliterating chunk of rock." That view of Newfoundland, by writer Wayne Johnston, is one that has greeted many a sailor, fisherman, traveller and settler as they have reached Canada after the Atlantic crossing.

The three Maritime provinces are New Brunswick, Nova Scotia, and Prince Edward Island. Though they occupy a large chunk of the early history of Canadian colonization, they make up only 1.4% of Canada's land area. Newfoundland and Labrador makes up another 4.1%. Together, there are 2.3 million people in the four Atlantic provinces, making up 7.6% of the national register.

The northerly Atlantic coastline, which lies in the same latitudes as the British Isles, is traced by the Labrador Current, flowing south from the Labrador Sea and transporting magnificent icebergs calved from the Greenland Ice Cap. These floating temporary exhibits of the Arctic can have calves of their own, known on the East Coast as 'growlers' or 'bergy bits.'

The Atlantic provinces offer a rugged edge to the saltwaters of the Atlantic and have been shaped by it. Every day, their waters inhale and exhale to the rhythm of the tides. Burntcoat Head, in the Bay of Fundy, has the largest tidal range in the world; in one day, the water level can rise and fall the height of a five-storey building.

Square-shaped New Brunswick, four-fifths of which is still forested, has one major island, Grand Manan Island. Nova Scotia has the much larger Cape Breton, which was joined to the mainland by the Canso Causeway in 1955. Prince Edward Island is Canada's only province completely surrounded by sea. It was reachable only by ferry until the 13-kilometre Confederation Bridge—the world's longest bridge spanning water that freezes over—connected it with New Brunswick in 1997.

The coastal Native peoples—the Micmac in the Maritimes and the Inuit in Labrador—have endured, and continue to sustain themselves from the sea, despite the arrival of so many successive waves of immigrants. The French-speaking Acadians were expelled from their homeland near the Bay of Fundy in the 1750s by the British during the wars between France and Britain. Many returned and have found their voice again. Maritimers understand that life by the ocean, like the sea itself, is restless but enduring.

Of Wind and Weather

"Aches and pain, coming rain" and "Seagull, seagull, sit on the sand, it's a sign of rain when you're at hand," are among the many weather maxims Canadians have to guide them in predicting precipitation—a pastime that can be considered a national sport. Mammals are also coerced into being weather vanes: the appearance or lack of a shadow of a rudely awakened groundhog—Wiarton Willie of Ontario—is used to decide the duration of winter.

However, should the seagulls or Willie be on break, Environment Canada offers Canadians the most prescient predictions of the weather to come. To paraphrase a radio-style update, courtesy of Environment Canada: "Cloudy today with intermittent rain. Possible hail toward evening. Sun tomorrow and for the weekend, rain."

Ice and snow —including thousands of glaciers of all sizes, 1,616 of them in the Nelson River drainage basin alone—are critical in the energy equation that dictates

"All I could see

was wind/turning the

brome grass/like the

hands of a clock/

round and round in

the dust/as if the earth

had asked/the wind

the time. Now"

Lorna Crozier,
Inventing the Hawk, 1992

29

Canadian weather. Acting as a blanket, they hold in heat at the same time as they reflect back incoming warmth. Like the canary in the mine, the state of the cryosphere is an indicator of climatic trends.

Although the lowest temperature ever recorded in Canada was a blood-freezing −63°C at Snag in the Yukon (February 3, 1947, the day after Groundhog Day), the Canadian climate is heating up. The decade of the 1990s was the warmest in recorded history, 1998 was the warmest year of the previous millennium, and the North is passing through a period of warming. One result is a reduction of northern sea ice in the Arctic by one-eighth over the last quarter-century, possibly making the Northwest Passage more navigable.

Wind and Water

Besides an abundance of land, Canada has wind and water aplenty. There is the power of Niagara Falls as it decants the waters of Lake Erie into Lake Ontario. There is Delta Falls in British Columbia, dropping 440 metres into the record books as Canada's tallest waterfall. There are mighty rivers, including Canada's longest, the 4,241–kilometre Mackenzie. There are also the five interconnected Great Lakes at the heart of Canada: Erie, Huron, Michigan, Ontario and Superior. By surface area, Lake Superior is the largest freshwater lake in the world. Our waterways are testimony to the extent and power of water in the Canadian landscape. Just under one-tenth, or 891,163 square kilometres of the total area of Canada, is freshwater, and at 14.7%, Ontario has the largest amount of its total area under water.

Harnessing our water resources to make power for home and business is an ongoing Canadian enterprise. The James Bay Project in northern Quebec, Canada's largest water control system, involved the initial construction of 215 separate dams.

Pioneer cabin near

Telkwa, British Columbia.

Photo by Lorne Clarke.

Walkerton, Ontario was a warning sign to guard against the contamination of community water supplies. This town of 5,000 on the Saugeen River experienced a fatal *e coli* contamination in 2000, and the disaster instigated improvements in water management across the country. The St. Lawrence River, once heavily tainted, has also experienced a co-ordinated reversal of its level of pollution, and Lake Ontario has a 'riverkeeper' program, where wardens patrol the waters on the lookout for threats to the lake's health.

The wind has many names in Canada. A chinook is known as a 'snow-eater' in the Prairies, and a 'cow storm' on Ellesmere Island is so called because it is proverbially strong enough to dehorn a muskox. The 'wreckhouse' wind of Newfoundland is self-explanatory.

Sometimes, we have mythologized the wind, sometimes our land, sometimes our cityscapes. The corner of Portage and Main in Winnipeg has been described as the windiest street corner in Canada. Often, the winds bring clear air from Canada's North, but sometimes, when they swing around from the south, they bear airborne pollutants. Environment Canada estimates 5,000 Canadians die annually from air pollution, and greenhouse gas emissions in Canada have risen 15% above 1990 levels.

Plants and Animals

Trees are good for us; of Canada's 134 native species, more than a quarter are considered to have medicinal uses. Chewing on willow bark might cure a headache, since it contains salicin, the active ingredient in acetylsalicylic acid. The venerable western yew tree found in British Columbia yields taxol, a compound that is used to treat cancer.

The Canadian roll call of flora and fauna is also important to our social and economic well-being. When surveyed in 1991, a full 86% of Canadians believed that our abundance of wildlife should be maintained. Almost the same proportion have long endorsed the protection of species under threat. *Wild Animals I Have Known* by naturalist Ernest Thompson Seton has been one of the bestselling Canadian books in our history since it was published in 1898.

Since 1842, when Charles Dickens visited Canada and wrote "the impression on my mind has been, from the first, nothing but Beauty and Peace," 12 Canadian wildlife species have become extinct. Another 16 species are no longer found in this country. It is the job of the Committee on the Status of Endangered Wildlife in Canada to monitor and report on the annual progress of native species and plants, from mammals to mosses. As of May 2001, a full 197 species were considered threatened or endangered; another 155 were designated 'of special concern.'

The *anatum* peregrine falcon has served as a mascot of the species protection movement and prompted concerted effort to save other endangered wildlife. The peregrine experienced a dramatic recovery after it was designated 'endangered' in 1978, received protection, and then was upgraded to 'threatened' in 2000. In 1941, only 21 whooping cranes were still alive in Canada. By 2001, the flock had grown to 177. There are also 204 captive birds maintained by a joint Canada–U.S. recovery team. In 1978, the prodigal swift fox was reintroduced into the Canadian wilderness—and it has stayed, one species among many thousands that consider Canada home turf.

"There is not a human being on earth so good but what personal acquaintance with our noble Canada goose will give him a desire to live better."

Jack Miner, 1927

I grew up in Esterhazy, Saskatchewan, a largely Hungarian settlement. Twelve miles down the road there's a town called Stockholm—guess who lives there. Nearby is St. Istvan, a Czech area. There were Finns in the Qu'Appelle Valley and Germans in Langenburg.

What makes all this work, I feel, are a few overarching, typically Canadian principles: a belief in tolerance, civility, democracy, a tradition of welcoming newcomers.

I am quietly but passionately proud to belong to such a country.

Guy Vanderhaeghe, writer

Yonge and Wellesley,

Toronto.

Photo by Pamela Harris.

THE PEOPLE

"We all live in small towns," writes Stuart McLean, broadcaster and author of the *Vinyl Cafe* stories. "Mine happens to be in the heart of a big city. It is Sam's corner store and Pasquale's bakery, Book City and the library down the street. The teachers who taught my boys this year. The parents who gather at the end of the arena for Saturday morning hockey. My neighbours, my haunts, my family, my home town."

For many of us, our worlds are of this smaller texture. Whether we gather in hockey arenas, coffee shops, grocery stores or at the bookstore, we've achieved a collection of 'Canadian' places that we recognize as home within the larger context of the city. Close to 8 in 10 of us—and we number 30 million—live in urban areas: Canada is a country of vast rural spaces, but we are mostly an urban people.

Canada's cities therefore bear dynamic witness to who we are as a people and whence we come. There are vivid and distinct architectures across the land—the balconies of Montréal's walk-ups, the brightly coloured saltbox houses of Atlantic Canada, and the Queen Anne revival homes in the older districts of Victoria or Winnipeg. In Ottawa, the National Gallery of Canada, an exhilarating glass and steel reflection of the creative spirit, shares a streetscape with the Royal Canadian Mint, an elegant stone and mortar reminder of an earlier age.

Undeniably, Canada is an immigrant nation. Walk the streets of any major city and our immigrant roots reveal themselves through our buildings, our cuisine and our faces. Of his street in Montréal—St. Urbain Street—Mordecai Richler once wrote, "Two streets below our own came the Main. Rich in delights…with something for all our appetites…[here] I was taken for a new suit…and shoes…We also shopped for fruit…meat and fish. [Here] too was the Chinese laundry…the Italian hatblocker…and strolling French Canadian priests."

Canadian society today stands as a microcosm of the entire world. People have come to settle here from nearly 190 countries around the world. Onion domes, church spires and minarets shape parts of our city skylines. The traditional tortière and Yorkshire pudding of our menus have been joined by the shawarma, chow mein, perogies, and sushi of successive waves of newcomers.

Even our First Nations tell stories of how their ancestors arrived from elsewhere—on the back of a turtle or by the trickery of Raven. The Norse landed at L'Anse aux Meadows in Newfoundland as early as 990. The French came in the early 1600s, well before Canada's founding. The British traders came around 1760. The United Empire Loyalists took up residence after the American Revolution, and the Scots and the Irish arrived in waves during the 1840s.

But the story really began to change and intensify shortly after Confederation, when Sir John A. Macdonald and his Conservative party came up with a blueprint for Canada called the National Policy. Under this plan, they would build a national railway that would tie the country together. They would advertise around the world, promising free land and drawing settlers to the yet untamed, vast stretches of the Canadian West.

By 1885, the 'last spike' had been driven into a transcontinental railway and in the years leading up to the First World War, immigrants began arriving in numbers unequaled before or since. In 1911 alone, Canada opened its gates to more than 330,000 immigrants; in 1913, to 400,000. In the 10 years leading up to the First World War, nearly 2.5 million immigrants landed in Canada. By 1914, Canada's population had reached nearly 8 million and almost 50% of us lived in cities.

Today, our numbers include the descendants of Russians, Austrians, Scandinavians, Scottish, English and Irish, as well as of black people who used the underground railway to escape slavery, Chinese people whose forefathers helped build Canada's first national railway and Japanese people who watched a world war from the confines of Canadian detention camps.

"Is this a happy

or a sad story?"

Betty Kennedy,
Front Page Challenge

41

In the 1960s, changes in our immigration policy removed many of the barriers to non-European immigrants. For at least the past decade, Asia has been the major source of newcomers to Canada; in fact, in 1996, about 21% of all visible minorities in Canada were South Asian and another 27% were Chinese. About 17% of Canadians have come from other countries. Those born in Europe were most likely to have come before 1971.

The majority (8 in 10) of visible minorities live in Canada's larger cities—Toronto, Montréal, Vancouver and Ottawa. In Toronto, for example, the Chinese are by far the largest visible minority, followed by South Asian and black people.

Recently, much attention has been paid to Canada's so-called 'brain drain,' particularly to the United States. However, the numbers in question are relatively small. In 1997, the number of Canadians who went to live permanently in the United States represented less than 1% of our work force. For every university graduate who goes south, four come to Canada from other lands. In fact, only once in the history of this nation—during the Great Depression in the 1930s—have those leaving outnumbered those arriving.

Canada, it would appear, has a long, strong history of being able to attract and keep people willing to take risks and make new beginnings.

Of Life and Aging

Although Canada is still a relatively young nation—135 years old in 2002—we are nonetheless aging as a people. In 1914, the average Canadian household was home to a lively 4.8 people, most of them young: some 33% of us were children, and only 5% were over 65. Today, the baby boomers, born during the two decades after the Second World War, are growing older, and only about 20% of Canadians are children younger than 15 years of age. The average household comprises just 2.6 people. Families are smaller and a far greater proportion of women work outside the home.

Today, there are about 3.9 million Canadians aged 65 and older who make up 13% of the population. By the year 2041, about 23% of all Canadians will be 65 and older. The fastest growth is occurring among older seniors, aged 85 and over: in 2001, an estimated 431,000 Canadians were aged 85 and over, more than double the number in 1981 and 20 times the number in 1921.

In fact, the life expectancy of seniors has risen substantially. A woman born in 1920 could expect to live 61 years and a man could see 59. A female born in the 1990s can expect to live to 81 years of age while a male can expect to make 75. The reason for the difference is this: men are more likely to suffer from diseases that kill relatively quickly, whereas women are more likely to suffer from diseases that are chronic and debilitating.

Not only are we an aging society, but our rate of growth has slowed as well. In every population, babies are born, old folks die, people move away and new people move in. In Canada, in the 12 months that ended in June 2001, more than 330,000 Canadians were born, 227,000 died, some 252,000 people arrived from other countries, and 65,000 picked up and left Canada. When demographers take all these numbers into account, they find Canada's growth rate to be lower than at any other time in our history, with the exception of the 1930s and the 1980s. In fact, for the first time in 100 years, our growth rate is lower than that of the United States.

At no other time in our history have Canadian women had fewer children: our rate of natural increase—based on a comparison of the number of births with the number of deaths—has been declining steadily for at least 10 years. As a result, between 1996 and 2001, immigrants accounted for more than half of our population's growth. Should current population trends continue and present immigration levels remain

"It is not uncertain prophecy, but sound deduction that the year 2000 will come on Canada with a population of 80 million."

George Johnson,
Commonwealth, 1901

Five generations.
Photo by Ted Grant,
CMCP.

First Communion.
Photo by Clara Gutsche,
CMCP.

Spruced.

Photo by David Trattles.

The War Brides "Many of the girls married 'glamorous, fly-by-night' soldiers and now, there they were, on a train moving across a foreign country in the dark of winter. Did their husbands still want them? How would their new in-laws react?…

"We let them off all the way west. Sometimes at whistle-stops at 3:00 a.m. and it would take hours to locate their trunks in the baggage-car. Everything they owned was in those trunks—blankets, clothing, cutlery, wedding gifts…

"The real shock was Calgary. We had sixteen spare brides. No one had shown up to claim them. Understandably, some of them were tearful and sorely in need of assurance that just because they hadn't been claimed, that didn't mean their husbands didn't love them. It just meant that they hadn't been properly informed about their arrival time."

This anonymous anecdote, from Ted Ferguson's *Sentimental Journey: An Oral History of Train Travel in Canada*, describes one of the most unusual waves of immigration in Canada's history—the war brides.

The first marriage between a British woman and a Canadian soldier

took place in England only 43 days after the Canadian troops landed in the United Kingdom in late 1939. Following the Second World War, nearly 45,000 women, many with young children, left behind their friends, families and ways of life to come to Canada as the wives of our soldiers. While the vast majority (93%) were British, many also came from the Netherlands, France, Belgium and Italy.

Like most immigrants in the postwar years, the majority of war brides arrived at Pier 21 in Halifax by transatlantic ship and then dispersed by rail to various destinations across the country. Over time, their stories of romance, journeys and spirit have become part of the cultural and historical tapestry of Canada.

In *The War Brides*, edited by Joyce Hibbert, a young bride recalls life in the bush: "At one time our home was an airplane packing case, measuring eight feet by forty, and we managed to make it into a liveable building. Two of our children were born while we lived there. Our 'home' was out in the bush, and we were surrounded by wild roses and saskatoon bushes. The beauty of it all made up for the rather strange living quarters."

Haarlem, the Netherlands, 1945. Courtesy of Lloyd and Olga Rains.

Hutterite boys.
Photo by
George Webber.

stable, Canada is projected to have negative population growth by 2046. Statistics Canada projects that, without immigrants, Canada's population would actually begin to decline by 2026.

Our Languages

In Michael Ondaatje's novel, *In The Skin of a Lion*, Nicholas is an immigrant who is able to speak only the native tongue of his homeland. After arriving in Canada, he goes to language school prior to working in bridge construction high above the ground. Ironically, writes Ondaatje, "for Nicholas language [was] much more difficult than what he [did] in space."

Nicholas' story describes well the difficulties that many new Canadians encounter. The numbers complete the picture: in 1998, about 290,000 people were enrolled in language schools to learn English or French. Nearly 4 in 10 were foreign students.

English and French, Canada's two official languages, are spoken at home by 69% and 23% of Canadians, respectively. Non-official languages, known as 'heritage languages,' are spoken in 11% of Canadian homes. Some of these languages are spoken by Aboriginal people, but most have been introduced by immigrants.

Indeed, a look at the language statistics tells us just how much the population's use of heritage languages has changed. In 1941, German and Ukrainian were the prevailing heritage languages in Canada. Today, Chinese is the most common heritage language, followed by Italian and German. Punjabi, Arabic and Tagalog are on the rise as we welcome more immigrants from India, the Middle East and the Philippines. Chinese is concentrated in Toronto and Vancouver, Italian in Montréal,

Portuguese in Kitchener, Ontario, and Tagalog, a language of the Philippines, in Winnipeg.

First Nations

This proud note figured in the 1996 Royal Commission report on Aboriginal Peoples:

"European peoples did not discover a vast and undeveloped land. They were welcomed with ceremony and protocol into the territories of nations. They did not encounter noble savages living in a state of nature. They came upon societies with ancient laws and cultures, peoples who each shared a language and a history, and who developed political and social structures beyond the level of kinship, clan or community."

Life, Beauty, Spirit,
1998.
Jane Ash Poitras,
Galerie d'Art Vincent.

Indeed, these societies were complex civilizations with extensive networks of trade and diplomacy. When the first Europeans arrived, Aboriginal people in what is now Canada spoke some 50 languages in 12 distinct language families. Today, about 3 in 10 Aboriginal people can still carry on a conversation in one of these languages.

In 1996, about 800,000 Canadians identified themselves as Aboriginal people. Some 69% were North American Indian, 26% were Métis, and 5% were Inuit. More than half of all these people lived in rural or remote areas, and just under 30% lived in metropolitan areas. Winnipeg is the city with the largest Aboriginal population—about 46,000 people, or 7% of the city's residents.

The Aboriginal population is generally younger than the total Canadian population. While Aboriginal people represent 3% of the Canadian population, Aboriginal children make up 5% of all Canadian children. In Manitoba and Saskatchewan, 20% of all children are Aboriginal.

Remote locations, high birthrates and sometimes unstable family life—fewer than 50% of Aboriginal children under the age of 15 live with both parents—have presented challenges for the education of Aboriginal children. School dropout rates are high, and only about 4% of the Aboriginal population over the age of 15 hold a university degree, compared with 19% of all Canadians. But the winds of change are blowing. Canada's only First Nations college, Saskatchewan Indian Federated College, has just celebrated its 25th anniversary, and the University of Saskatchewan currently enrolls 2,300 Aboriginal students—more than any other Canadian campus.

Home Life

"The rent was forty-five dollars a month; my weekly salary then was no more than fifty," recalls writer Pierre Berton of moving to an apartment in Vancouver as a newly-wed in 1946. "Our bachelor apartment was so small that when the Murphy bed was pulled down from the wall it filled the room. The kitchen wasn't much bigger than a broom closet."

As much as we may begin married life in modest rentals with Murphy beds, for most Canadians, owning a home, however plain, is part of our dream and the single most important investment we will make in our lifetime; even more important than holding a Registered Retirement Savings Plan.

Mortgages on Canadian homes account for more than 75% of homeowner debt while 36% of all households choose to rent. Close to 56% of households consist of single detached houses, and more than 30% are apartments. Most residents say their homes provide good shelter. Over 75% of Canadian householders say their home is in no need of repair; a further 16% say only minor repairs are needed.

In Canada, our housing seems to have an impact upon the level of contact that we have with other people in our villages, neighbourhoods and hometowns. In 1996, about 8 in 10 residents living in single detached dwellings interacted with neighbours. This fell to 7 in 10 for people in duplexes and row houses, and to 6 in 10 for those in apartments.

Folks on rural routes interact more with neighbours than do people in urban areas. Husband–wife families are likely to have more social contact than lone-parent families or people living alone, and seniors socialize significantly more than young adults.

The wish to live in some form of community remains a constant in Canadian life; some 85% of us live in family households, whereas fewer than 10% live alone. Yet, many of the social ties that traditionally connect us are dissolving. If marriage in the legal sense has formalized our romances, we often now find its promise soured and we call it a day. Yet, we find togetherness increasingly outside of formal unions, once more trying for an ideal—the security and comfort of family life.

In 1968, the *Divorce Act* introduced the idea of no-fault as grounds for marriage breakdown and, within the space of two short decades, Canada's divorce rate had shot to a staggering 362 couples for every 100,000 people. To give this historical perspective, in 1921, the divorce rate was 6.4, a number that doubled to 14.3 in 1936. Following the Second World War, the divorce rate rose to 63.1, but then it dropped again to 37.6 by 1951.

Despite the risks the numbers bespeak, Canadians continue to forge unions both within and outside formal legal marriage. Today, about a third of all married couples eventually call it quits; the 1998 divorce rate was 228 for every 100,000 people. At the same time, so many young couples now set up house without marrying that by

"That house in Manawaka is the one which, more than any other, I carry with me…it was plain as the winter turnips in its root cellar."

Margaret Laurence
A Bird in the House, 1970

Mom and daughter
on rocks.
Photo copyright
Peter Sibbald, 1998.

Zappy Red Riding
Hood.
Photo copyright
Peter Sibbald, 1998.

2020, there may well be as many common-law unions in Canada as there are marriages. Nor are common-law unions insurance against the *sturm und drang* of break-up. Half of all couples within a common-law union find themselves calling it off within five years, and women in their 30s and 40s who live common law and then marry their partners are almost twice as likely to separate or divorce as those who marry without first living together.

The nuclear family of earlier days, Mom, Dad, three youngsters and the dog, has now given way to an assortment of unions and not surprisingly, many more babies are now born outside of formal marriage. The rise of the blended family now takes its place front and centre along with lone-parent and two-parent families, while nearly 9% of Canadian children live in a step-family.

Between 1981 and 1991, the proportion of people reporting no religious affiliation rose from 7% to 13%. While monthly attendance at religious services is down substantially over the past decade, about 34% of adults report they attend services at least once a month. Older Canadians, immigrants and people living in rural areas or small towns have higher rates of participation in religious activities.

Urban Landscapes

"Canada is a brown trout in a field of mint…Canada is a crow on a highway," wrote Dennis Tourbin in 1992 in his visual poetic "Canada Is." A.J. Casson spent much of the 20th century painting a tranquil portrait of Canada's rural villages— pictures of white clapboard houses, crimson maples and tangled gardens. From A.J. Casson to Charles Gagnon, from Nicole Brossard to Eleanor Bond have come many personal and poetic visions of our urban and rural landscapes. If it is true, however, that artists reflect the reality of our everyday lives, many of their visual messages must now reflect a post-industrial reality, a consequence of the great surge of Canadians toward our cities and away from our small towns and countryside.

Then Again The passage of time has many measures: the waxing and waning of the moon, the calendar, stiffening joints and at "the beginning of the long dash, following 10 seconds of silence, [it will be] exactly one o'clock…" Mavis Gallant, the Canadian writer, once wrote that the watch continues to tick even when the story has stopped.

Timely conceits aside, time's companion—change—has been consistent and constant in Canada since our official story began in 1867. Some smattering of statistics accompanied the launch of the nation, as the first *Canada Year Book*, also published in 1867, attests. A more nuanced picture, however, began to unfold at the turn of the century. Here's what we find:

In 1900, women made up about 13% of Canada's work force. Today, they make up 46%. At the turn of the century, they held not a single seat in Canada's House of Commons. Today, they hold 62 out of a possible 301. In 1900, they gave birth to an average 4.6 babies; today, just 1.6. Not surprisingly, the average household ran to a rather busy five people; today, it's 2.6. Then, some 12% of university students were women; today, that's up to 55%.

When the telephone rang in 1900, it could not have been in any more than about 52,000 homes. Today, there are roughly 23 million phones in Canadian households and that doesn't include the trill of the ubiquitous cell.

On the other hand, if one relished the quackish honk of an early Model T, one had little chance of hearing it in 1900. There were only 178 cars registered—all of them in Ontario. Today, there are more than 14 million.

There seemed to be a pugilistic streak among early Canadian sportifs. In 1900, boxing was one of the most popular sports, second only to baseball and just ahead of lacrosse. Today, it's golf, ice hockey and baseball in that order.

One could write a love letter in 1900 and spend two cents on a postage stamp. Today, it would cost 48 cents. Then again, the average wage in 1900 was $308 a year. Today, it's $23,000 for women and $35,000 for men.

Most of us lived in the country—63%. Today, most of us live in cities—80%. Then again, at the turn of the century, our cities were not the bustling mega-urban centres they are today. We were beginning, and for Canada, the beginning was on the land.

Suburban malls and hockey rinks are the new town squares of our society: we meet here as we once met at the drugstore soda fountains of small Canadian towns and villages. We increasingly embrace city life. Since 1951, the proportion of Canadians living in rural areas has fallen from 43% to just over 20% in 2001, and 64% of Canadians live in large metropolitan settings of 100,000 people or more.

Most of us live "on the fender of the American border," as Stephen Leacock quipped more than half a century ago, and this continues to hold true. Most of us live within 200 kilometres of the United States. In fact, 22% of all Canadians are clustered in a sprawling sweep of cities, which includes the Golden Horseshoe and which extends several hundred kilometres around the southwestern end of Lake Ontario. The population of Greater Toronto alone—4.7 million people—is more than four times that of the entire province of Manitoba.

Between 1996 and 2001, the extended Golden Horseshoe—a mere speck of 11,900 square kilometres within Canada's total area of some 10 million square kilometres—accounted for almost 50% of Canada's population growth. Yet even here, the frontier is never too far away. In a country as large as Canada, urban dwellers seldom have to travel great distances to find what W.O. Mitchell described as "all that land and all that sky."

Moving Day

In the 1950s, at the age of 20, a young Inuit woman named Minnie Aodla Freeman moved from Cape Hope Island in James Bay to Ottawa to work as a translator. In *Life Among the Qallunaat*, she tells the story of her move:

Precious cargo.

Photo by Mike Beedell.

"I had paid little attention to the names of the streets, but would go by the shapes of stores or commercial signs. Such was how I had learned to find my way in my culture...Passing the Chateau Laurier every day I saw a big sign...and knew that I was heading in the right direction. But one day, the sign was gone and suddenly all the buildings looked the same to me."

Minnie finally found her way with the help of a friendly policeman, but her story goes far in telling us this: whichever direction we go, our moves across this vast land are significant personal events that find their way into our writings and even our songs. And we do move about; in the year ending June 30, 2000 alone, nearly 1.3 million people moved to a new address in Canada.

Over 40% of Canada's population—and we now surpass 30 million—will change dwellings every five years. Some of us will pick up and move across the country, whereas others will just cross the street. Some of us will move for family reasons, others to find work, and still others for that ineffable feeling of finding a home.

Indeed, one of the compelling truths about Canada is that so many of our early pioneers came in search of just that—a home. Answering the call of a newly forming nation hungry for citizens, they came from the four corners of the earth. One could almost say the spirit of venturing is imprinted in Canada's history.

Today, most of us do not stray far from our own small corners however, often exchanging one address for another just around the corner or out in that new sub-division by the highway.

Incidentally, Minnie was part of a generation that changed the direction of migration. Earlier in the 20th century, more people moved from Ontario to other provinces.

Following the industrial boom of the 1940s and 1950s, more people headed to Ontario than moved away. In the last decade, the star destination has been British Columbia; since the late 1990s, more Canadians have been Alberta bound.

Canada Giving

The history of volunteering in Canada is as old as the country itself. In fact, it predates Confederation: as early as 1639, the Hospitaller Sisters managed the first medical mission in New France, coming to the aid of the Iroquois. Canada's pioneering families survived largely because they helped one another overcome the rigours of the Canadian climate and the difficulties of building new homes and lives in a foreign country.

In 1885, a militia force set out from Central Canada to quell the Northwest Rebellion, which raged across what is now the Prairie provinces. Among the force was George Sterling Ryerson, who used a makeshift red cross to identify his horse-drawn ambulance as safe haven for those wounded in battle. In 1896, he went on to found the Canadian Red Cross Society, which has extended its work of helping people throughout the world.

In Canada today, a full 27% of adults volunteer their time, down from 31% in 1997. Of the total, 54% are women. In 2000, Canadians spent the equivalent of 549,000 full-time jobs on volunteer activities, but the effort was not evenly distributed. "If you need a job done, find someone who is busy" runs the old adage, and it seems to aptly describe the volunteer sector. The most active 25% of volunteers supplied almost 75% of all the time donated. Seniors are the biggest players; they average about 269 hours a year, more than double the hours given by young adults aged 15 to 24.

"Among the force was George Sterling Ryerson, who used a makeshift Red Cross to identify his horse-drawn ambulance..."

From the story of the Canadian Red Cross

61

Another adage, "time is money," seems also to fit the volunteer profile. In 2000, some 91% of adult Canadians donated money or goods to charitable and non-profit organizations. However, a relatively small proportion of people gave the most: fewer than 10% of all donors gave 46% of the dollar value of all contributions, estimated at more than $5 billion. Those with university degrees and seniors made the highest average donations.

While the Canadian penchant for giving of one's time and money is relatively high, recent trends show a decline in volunteering and giving time. Between 1997 and 2000, the number of donors, the number of volunteers and the number of hours given all fell, despite an increase in the general population. Only the total dollar value of donations increased.

Much of the good will of Canadians is expressed through religious institutions and groups. In 2000, these organizations received almost half of all donated dollars and one-fifth of all volunteered time.

Giving and helping varies widely across Canada, no doubt a reflection of economic circumstances, social values, cultural conventions and social milieu. People in the Prairie and Atlantic provinces were more likely to give to charitable causes, but people in Manitoba and Alberta gave the largest donations. Volunteering was highest in the Prairie provinces and Prince Edward Island, but people in the Atlantic provinces generally contributed the most time.

Red Cross poster.
Work by Stapleton,
Canadian War Museum,
AN19720114-023.

I am a walker.

In my travels through Canada, I walk the cities and their museums, gathering images. Eaton's in Winnipeg. The CPR hotel in Vancouver. A long, white limousine in Toronto. Stones in the water near Stanley Park.

I take much from these images; they connect me to intense feelings which make their way into my poetry and my novels.

In a way, I am an explorer and Canada is one of my places of exploration.

Nicole Brossard, writer

Kingsmere.
Photo by
J. David Andrews,
Masterfile.

THE SOCIETY

In 1864, George Brown, one of Canada's founding fathers and a key delegate to the Charlottetown Conference in Prince Edward Island, wrote to his wife: "On Friday we met in Conference and Canada opened her batteries—John A. and Cartier exposing the general arguments in favour of Confederation—and this occupied the time until the hour of adjournment at three. At four o'clock Mr. Pope gave us a grand *déjeuner à la fourchette.*"

The formal dinner appears to have relaxed the conference delegates. Brown's sense of triumph sails toward us 138 years later: "Cartier and I made eloquent speeches —of course—and whether as the result of our eloquence or of the goodness of our champagne, the ice became completely broken, the tongues of the delegates wagged merrily, and the banns of matrimony between all the Provinces of BNA…[were] there-upon formally completed and proclaimed!"

Three years later, in 1867, the 'marriage' was solemnized, and the new Dominion of Canada came into being. It was a formal confederation of three colonies—New Brunswick, Nova Scotia and Canada (the union of Upper and Lower Canada)—with a federal parliament made up of the Monarch (represented by the Governor General), an appointed senate and an elected house of commons. The colonies became four provinces—Ontario, Quebec, New Brunswick and Nova Scotia—each with its own lieutenant-governor and legislative assembly.

But more than these outward forms, the new Canada held the promise of a nation that would one day stretch "*A Mari usque ad Mare* / From Sea to Sea." Although several colonies chose not to join at the time, the Charlottetown delegates might have delighted in Joey Smallwood's words some 80 years later. As the Premier of Newfoundland, Canada's last holdout to Confederation, Smallwood admitted that "the only thing wrong with Confederation is that we didn't join in 1867." Today, Canada extends across 10 provinces and three territories to the shores of three oceans.

For the Fathers of Confederation, power would be distilled and distributed between the federal government and the provinces. As these founding members watched a civil war tear apart the United States in the 1860s, they became determined to assign broad national powers to the federal government, and more local issues—health and education, for instance—to the provinces. Some matters, such as immigration and agriculture, were to be shared by both. This complex system, unique to Canada, has often been cited as a reflection of our genius for compromise.

Thus, when the delegates at the Charlottetown Conference debated the general purposes of the laws that their new Parliament would make, their minds did not turn to ringing declarations of liberty, equality and brotherhood, or of life, liberty and the pursuit of happiness. Instead, they chose 'peace, order and good government.'

Today, their decisions have evolved into a system that serves Canada well, although it might sometimes seem that our national conversation is dominated by the issue of jurisdiction. As the journalist Michael Valpy once wryly noted, "Canada is the only country in the world where you can buy a book on federal–provincial relations at an airport."

As the 21st century begins, some 2.8 million people—about 17% of Canada's total labour force—assumed governance of our federal, provincial, territorial and municipal governments as well as the running of the education, health and justice sectors. In 2001, these governments together spent more than $417 billion to provide Canadians with a range of services from garbage collection to issuing passports.

The Law

"The purpose of law is to turn passion to reason," wrote the lawyer and poet, F.R. Scott and Pierre Elliott Trudeau took 'Reason over Passion' to be his personal maxim. But do we, as a nation, succeed these maxims? The statistics are helpful, but not conclusive.

"There's only so much national mythology that can be created in 135 years. Relax."

Douglas Coupland,
Souvenir of Canada, 2002

Pierre Elliott Trudeau.

1919–2000.

Photo by

Jean-Marc Carisse.

In 2000, our overall reported crime rate dropped for the ninth year in a row, reaching its lowest level since 1978. For every 100 Canadians, eight incidents of crime are now reported. In 1991, for every 100 Canadians, 10 incidents were reported.

There may be many reasons for this: changes in legislation, shifts in police enforcement or changes in the willingness of victims to report crime. One thing is clear, however: ours is an aging population and older people are simply less likely to engage in crime. Undoubtedly, for similar reasons, homicide rates have also fallen in many other countries where populations are aging, such as in the United States, France, Italy and Germany.

While the overall crime rate refers to all types of crime, whether homicide, assault or theft, the violent crime rate includes homicide, attempted murder, assault and kidnapping or abduction. In this instance, there has actually been a recent and slight increase, caused by a rise in the number of assaults. Still, violent crimes made up 13% of the 2.6 million crimes charged under Canada's *Criminal Code* in 2000. In 1966, they made up 10% of more than 700,000 crimes.

Over the last 20 years, we have consistently recorded lower rates of violent crime than has the United States. Our incidence of homicide, the most serious of crimes, was less than two for every 100,000 people in 2000, one-third that of the United States, and our lowest rate since 1967.

Murder, unfortunately, is often a crime chillingly close to home: more than 50% of all victims die in their own homes at the hands of someone they know. Most at risk of being a victim of homicide are infants under one year of age: 9 of the 20 infants killed in 2000 died after being shaken by a parent or caregiver.

In the United States, two out of every three homicides involve a gun. In Canada, only one in three such deaths involves a firearm. Gang-related homicides have more than tripled since 1995, and now account for one murder victim in every eight.

In 1999, some 5% of all Canadians were victims of violent crime. The possibility of being victimized increases substantially for people who are young, male, single and living on a low income. Contrary to what some people may assume, living in a city does not increase the risk of violent crime. Homicide rates in the city, for example, are very similar to those in towns, villages and rural areas.

Property crimes, such as fraud or breaking and entering, are also down from 1991. Since 1981, the number of people charged with driving under the influence of alcohol has dropped by 57%.

Most Canadians think our police forces do a good job, but we are less likely to view the criminal courts and the prison and parole systems with equal favour. Survey results are ambiguous; while more of us feel satisfied with our overall safety, there is still a tense feeling among 30% of us: this group feels that crime is up.

In 2000, of the 220,600 adult suspects who were admitted into custody, almost 89,000 were eventually sentenced to custody in provincial, territorial or federal institutions and another 73,000 adults to probation. The number of Aboriginal people sentenced to custody, however, continues to be out of proportion to the general population. Although Aboriginal people represent just 2% of the adult Canadian population, in 2000, they made up fully 17% of the adults in custody in federal, provincial and territorial institutions.

The Scales of Justice

The Canadian justice system employs two kinds of law, reflecting our French and English heritage. Common law, which is used in all provinces except Quebec, can be traced back to medieval England and relies on court judgments as precedents. The civil law of Quebec dates back even further, to the consolidation of Roman law by Emperor Justinian; in civil law, a written code (*code civil*) is more important than precedents in guiding judges' decisions.

In Canada, each province is responsible for establishing its own courts to deal with matters arising under both federal and provincial law.

Although provincial court judges are appointed by the provinces, the federal government names superior court judges, who preside over the highest courts in the provinces and territories. Superior courts not only hear more serious cases than do the provincial courts; they also have the power to review lower court decisions.

The Supreme Court of Canada serves as Canada's final court of appeal. In recognition of Quebec's civil law system, three of the nine judges must be from that province. As a result of the *Canadian Charter of Rights and Freedoms,* which became part of our Constitution in 1982, the Supreme Court has many more cases before it. Between 1990 and 2000, the number of cases filed before the Supreme Court increased by 36% to 659.

In 2000, some 23% of all appeals heard by the Supreme Court were filed under the *Canadian Charter of Rights and Freedoms.* Charter cases have, in fact, continued to increase in all courts because the Charter, as part of the 1982 *Constitution Act,* makes the protection of human rights fundamental. Unlike previous human rights legislation, which was in the form of statutes, the Charter cannot be repealed.

In 2000–01, Canada's federal, provincial and municipal governments spent $32.6 billion on the justice system, or about $1,086 for every man, woman and child in Canada. Policing costs were the single biggest item that year, averaging almost $221 for each Canadian, or about 21% of the total.

Education

"I have never lost the sense," wrote the literary philosopher Northrop Frye, "that the university is very near the centre of the idea of human community, and that our society stands or falls with it." Academic and journalist Arnold Edinborough once told a graduating class, "A university should provide you with one thing at least—a reading list for the rest of your life."

Commitment to education is one of the cornerstones of Canadian thinking. In 1998, our investment in education, as a proportion of gross domestic product (GDP), was among the top G7 countries.

"After all the heart is not a small stone/ to be rolled this way and that./ The mind is not a box/ to be shut fast."

Anne Carson,
The Beauty of the Husband,
2002

But funds are only one side of the education picture in Canada. This is a country where teaching styles go in and out of fashion. In the early days, most students attended the so-called little red schoolhouses. The curricula featured the 'three R's' —reading, writing and 'rithmetic—with a smattering of geography and the sciences. Generally, a single teacher ruled the classroom and not infrequently, the strap could be produced as a way of ensuring the rule was kept.

But by the 1950s, 1960s and 1970s, the little red schoolhouse had become a thing of the past. Larger, urban creations housed many classrooms, labs and gym facilities and could educate many hundreds of students at once.

Teaching methods are also changing. Throughout the land, schoolchildren now also sit in front of computer terminals, chasing down a range of subjects on the Internet. The tap-tap sound of the keyboard has, at least partly, replaced the scratch of pens across old-style school-issue scribblers. Today, students in the farthest outreaches of Canada can follow courses given in the largest of city centres. There's been a move toward standardized testing. At the same time, there are the ongoing challenges of our time: many school boards have had to do with fewer resources and many highly experienced teachers will retire over the next few years.

Despite our shifting pedagogical styles and perhaps because of them, Canada ranks highly with regard to educational accomplishment. In 1996, more than 48% of Canadians aged 25 to 64 had some post-secondary education, compared with the OECD average of 23%. Collectively, we spent about $66.3 billion on education in 2000–01. Of this, a good 60% went to elementary and secondary schools and the rest to colleges and universities.

In 2000, about one million Canadians were enrolled in Canada's 100 universities and 200 technical schools and community colleges, and about one-third of them were part-time students.

The dancers.
Photo by Glen Jones,
Images International.

Historically, women have been less likely than men to pursue university studies, but not so today. Today, they make up about 55% of the student population, up from 37% in the mid-1970s and up immeasurably from the early to mid-part of this century. In fact, women now form the majority of students in Canada's community colleges and have for more than 20 years.

In the last 10 years, tuition costs have more than doubled for the average undergraduate student from $1,500 at the beginning of the 1990s to $3,380 in 2000–01. It is true that young people from low-income families are less likely to enrol in a college or university than are those from families with higher incomes.

Our pedagogy seems to stand our students in good stead. In 2000, in a major international test, Canadian 15-year-olds ranked among the best in the world in reading, science and mathematics. Of the 32 countries involved, only students from Finland scored better than Canadians at reading. Within Canada, students from Alberta led all other provinces, especially in reading ability. The news was also good in science and math, with Canadian students ranking fifth and sixth, respectively. Incidentally, Canada ranked sixth in the proportion of GDP spent on elementary and secondary education, compared with other Organisation for Economic Co-operation and Development (OECD) countries.

Canadian youngsters are now more apt to stay in school. Our drop-out rate is down and many more young Canadians are off to university. In fact, Canada's labour force is one of the most educated among OECD countries, with fully 50% of Canadian workers with a degree, diploma or certificate.

Still, some 26% of all Canadian adults can deal with only simple reading and writing tasks. Among seniors, approximately 40% have not completed primary school, and more than 1.6 million possess poor literacy skills.

Education is not the only predictor of literacy. In fact, about 20% of Canadians are less literate, and a further 16% more literate, than their levels of education might suggest. For example, young people who are regular readers and letter writers have been shown to be considerably more literate than those who are not.

Health

"Had I been a rich man's son," said Tommy Douglas, speaking of a childhood medical crisis, "the services of the finest surgeons would have been available. As an iron moulder's boy, I almost had my leg amputated before chance intervened and a specialist cured me without thought of a fee. All my adult life I have dreamed of the day when an experience like mine would be impossible and we would have in Canada a program of complete medical care without a price tag."

In 1947, under Douglas's leadership, Saskatchewan became the first province to establish universal public hospital insurance. Over the next several years, the other provinces and territories would follow suit, until physicians' services across the country, both in and out of hospitals, were covered by the state.

Today, however, Canadians are engaged in a fierce and on-going national debate on how to maintain Canada's health care system. Until now, the idea of free and universal medical care for all has been one of the linchpins of national social policy. In fact, for many, its existence has been one of the guiding values of our national policy and what makes us distinctly 'Canadian.'

But, the challenges we face as a nation have changed and thus has this fundamental value been challenged. The reasons are plaintive, financial and geographic: we are an aging population, and many of the new medical technologies come with enormous price tags. We have pockets of settlement far away in our North and thus, far from the hospitals of our big cities. Some believe the private sector should provide more health services, others argue for user fees, and many still hold firm to the idea of universal state-paid medical care.

Not surprisingly, the rhythms of health care have altered dramatically. Our hospital stays are shorter. In 1998, there were almost three times as many outpatient services as in 1985 and the number of hospital beds dropped by 25% over the same period.

"A cool, clean place, is how she thinks of it, with a king and queen and Mounties wearing red jackets and people drinking tea."

Carol Shields,
The Stone Diaries, 1993

Auntie Ilfra, 1997.
Work by Rosalie Favell,
Indian Art Centre,
Indian and Northern
Affairs Canada.

Visits to hospital emergency rooms are up, the waits are longer and there are more clinics. Since the early 1990s, private sector funding of health care through supplemental insurance and out-of-pocket health care expenses has grown at roughly the same rate as public sector spending. Today, about 72% of health care services are publicly funded.

Nonetheless, Canada places high on the list of countries investing significantly in health care. In 1998, for example, Canada ranked third among G7 countries, behind the United States and Germany, in terms of expenditure per person. In 2000, Canada spent $95 billion—about $3,000 for every man, woman and child—on health care. Overall, Canadian governments spend about twice as much on health as they do on justice.

Health Culprits

Three health culprits confound our well-being and are major causes of death in Canada: circulatory disease, cancer and respiratory disease. Lung cancer deaths are 80% higher among men than women. Though female smoking rates are dropping, they are not dropping nearly as sharply as those of men.

Canadians continue to look beyond traditional Western health-care methods to available alternatives. In 1998–99, some 17% of Canadians went off to see practitioners such as chiropractors, massage therapists, acupuncturists, homeopaths and naturopaths.

Generally speaking, the health of First Nations and Inuit people does not compare well with the health of other Canadians. In 1996, their mortality rate was about 1.5 times higher than the national rate except in Alberta and Quebec, and they were up to 6.5 times more likely to die of injuries and poisonings than the rest of

A Smoking Story A silver cigarette case snaps open to reveal a row of tidily constructed cigarettes within. One is removed, tapped on a nearby table edge and a lighter flares. The camera pans back, the protagonist inhales deeply and the director says, "Cut. It's a wrap."

Such 'cigarette moments' of the cinema once sent a powerful message to moviegoers—smoking is glamourous, exciting even. Today, however, the story line has changed. If someone does light up in a movie scene, it may be to signal anxiety or Serious Trouble Brewing.

With good cause. In Canada, cigarette smoking accounts for 90% of new lung cancer cases in men and 80% in women. In 2001, nearly 16,000 men and women died of lung cancer caused by cigarette smoking—more than the entire population of Camrose, Alberta, or Bracebridge, Ontario, or Bathurst, New Brunswick.

The good news, however, is that smoking rates in Canada have hit their lowest rates in 36 years. For example, in 1965, when the first study of tobacco use was conducted, fully 50% of Canadians smoked. Today, this is down to 23%. Mostly, it's young adults in their early 20s who tend to smoke, but even in this group the rate is down: 34% today compared to 49% in 1981.

Dear Jared, 1979.
Work by
Barbara Astman,
The Robert
McLaughlin Gallery.

Canadians. Although Aboriginal life expectancy in 1995 had increased to 69 years for men and 76 years for women, these figures were still disturbingly below the comparable ages of 75 and 81, respectively, for other Canadians.

Governance

Since the earliest days of New France, Canada has been a monarchy. The Fathers of Confederation were very clear that they wanted executive power in the new nation to be exercised in the name of the Sovereign, the Queen of Canada, as our head of state. Ever since, all government actions have been taken by the Crown.

In 2002, Queen Elizabeth II celebrated the Golden Jubilee of her ascension to the throne. Coincidentally, in 1952, Vincent Massey was the first Canadian to be appointed Governor General. Many of our 26 governors general since Confederation have had distinguished careers in the military, politics or literature. For example, while in office from 1935 to 1940, John Buchan, Lord Tweedsmuir, wrote popular fiction, such as *The Thirty-Nine Steps*, as well as his memoirs and instituted the Governor General's Literary Awards in 1936.

Although the governor general retains certain prerogative powers—appointing and dismissing prime ministers, granting pardons, summoning and dissolving Parliament, for example—, he or she must usually act on ministerial advice and confine comments on public policy to what has been humourously dubbed the 'governor-generalities.'

The most powerful office in the land, that of the prime minister, was not even mentioned in the *Constitution Act, 1867*, as the original *British North America Act* is now known. The prime minister, normally the leader of the largest political party in the House of Commons, does not necessarily have to be a member of the House. Sir John Abbott, the first Canadian-born Prime Minister (1891–92) was a Senator, as was Sir Mackenzie Bowell (1894–96).

Carnaval de Montréal,
1885,
Musée de la civilisation,
Québec, 88-403.

The prime minister governs with the assistance of cabinet ministers, who are in charge of federal departments. Public servants advise these ministers and carry out the day-to-day administration of governance. In the United States, the executive and legislative branches of government are quite separate; under Canada's parliamentary system, they are fused together. The independence of the judiciary, however, is very carefully preserved.

Most proposed legislation can be introduced as a bill in either the House of Commons or the Senate. But to become law—an Act of Parliament—it must be passed by both houses of Parliament and receive royal assent from the governor general or a delegate, or in special ceremonial cases from the Monarch.

The provinces have similar processes for passing laws, except that they do not have the equivalent of the Senate, and the government leader is usually called the Premier (Prime Minister, in Quebec). The lieutenant-governor of a province gives royal assent to provincial acts.

On the Agenda

For each new session of Parliament, the government sets out its agenda in the Speech from the Throne, read by the governor general or, in special instances, by the Queen.

In the speech opening the 37th Parliament on January 30, 2001, the government agenda focussed on innovation, including a commitment to make Canada one of the top five countries in research and development by 2010 and a promise to help

Lady Elizabeth Bowes-Lyon, aged 4, with brother David. Photo by ILN/Camera Press/PonoPresse.

The Queen Mother, 1900–2002. Photo by Anthony Buckley, Camera Press/PonoPresse.

one million adult Canadians gain new skills and knowledge. The government also announced plans to modernize privacy and copyright laws, work with the provinces to improve child-support laws, increase funding for the Canadian Institutes of Health Research, provide better law-enforcement tools to deal with cybercrime and terrorism, and increase funds for the Canadian Forces.

As baby boomers move toward retirement, 75% of today's senior government managers will have chaired their last meeting by 2011, so it is not surprising that for government, an on-going concern is attracting qualified people to work in the public service. In 1998, the number of public sector workers expanded for the first time in four years. In 2001, government services was the only sector in which demand accelerated and jobs increased.

There has also been concern that fewer Canadians have been exercising their right to vote. Between the 1940s and 1980s, voter turnout in federal general elections ranged between 73% and 78%. In 1997, election officials noted a downturn, when only 67% of registered electors voted. In November 2000, the trend continued, with only 61% choosing to vote.

The irony is that while we are better educated, with push-button access to more information, our attachment to traditional political parties has weakened over the past decade, and this makes it less likely that we will vote. In 2001, almost one-third of voters also believed that there was no single important campaign issue, a perception that may have decided some against voting. In the 1988 general election, which was fought on the issue of free trade, more than 75% of eligible Canadians exercised their electoral right, which adds support to the notion that without a single important campaign issue, involvement flags.

North Rustico, P.E.I.

Photo by John Sylvester.

We Are a Song... In 1927, Judge Emily Murphy wrote: "Canada is not a map, not a government…No! Canada is a theme; it is a tune, and it must be sung together…"

This writer and pioneering magistrate had much to address in the emancipation of Canadian women; up until 1929, women were still not considered 'persons' in the eyes of the law.

On the other hand, their ability to serve as judges, at least in the province of Alberta, had been recognized in 1916, with the appointment of Murphy herself as a magistrate—the first female magistrate in the British Empire. The move did not create concordant songs, however, in the hearts of male litigators: they objected to appearing before a woman judge because women were, after all, not legally 'persons'.

Undaunted, Judge Murphy enlisted four Albertan women activists —Louise McKinney, Nellie McClung, Irene Parlby and Henrietta Muir Edwards—and together the 'Famous 5' launched the Persons Case to change the law.

In October 18, 1929, the Judicial Committee of the Privy Council of the British House of Lords, at that time Canada's highest court, ruled unanimously that women were indeed 'persons' and eligible for appointment to the Senate.

Louise McKinney

NA-825-1

Nellie McClung

NA-273-2

Emily Murphy

NA-273-3

Irene Parlby

NA-273-1

Henrietta Muir Edwards

NA-2607-1

'Famous 5'

Glenbow Archives,

Calgary, Alberta.

Yoho National Park,
British Columbia.
Photo by
Hélène Anne Fortin.

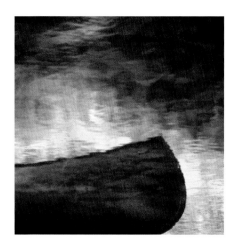

I grew up in Middle Cove just outside St. John's. Humour was big in our family and humour is very important in Newfoundland. You don't get far here unless you can make people laugh.

I grew up watching the Wonderful Grand Band, which was a weekly comedy show produced out of St. John's. It was great because it was Newfoundlanders doing comedy about Newfoundland. It gave me the confidence to go on to become a comedian.

I knew that what we had right here at home was just as good or better than anything that might come "through the narrows."

Rick Mercer, comedian

Chan Hon Goh.
Photo by J. Ciancio,
The National Ballet
of Canada.

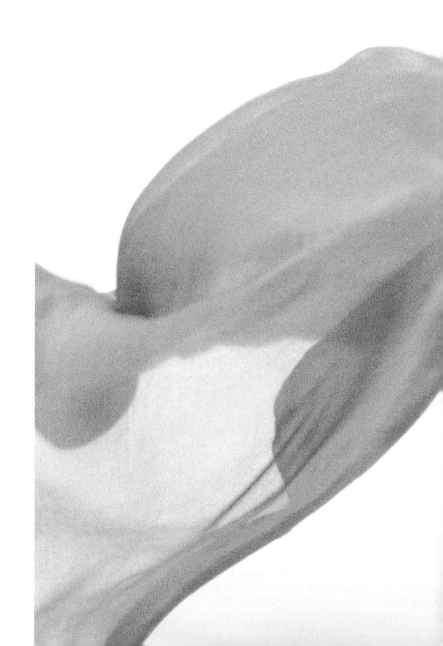

ARTS AND LEISURE

The year was 1982, and tiny Baie-Saint-Paul, Quebec was hosting one of its many artistic festivals. It was there that a group of young street performers, calling themselves *le Club des talons hauts* walked among the crowds on towering stilts, juggling and eating fire. Inspired by the obvious delight of the spectators, the performers hatched the idea of a festival to be called *La Fête foraine de Baie-Saint-Paul*. Twenty years later, the *Cirque du Soleil*, as it was to become, charms some seven million people a year with eight troupes performing on two continents.

Some decades ago, during the 1940s and 50s, modernism, surrealism and automatism in the visual arts provoked widespread controversy in Quebec. Paul-Émile Borduas and other artists authored the *Refus global* in 1948, a manifesto that rejected not only traditional artistic concepts but also the religious and political establishment of the time.

When Zacharias Kunuk was about four or five years old, living in a one-room sod house in the far North, he remembers his parents telling him the story of *Atanarjuat* —"the fast runner." That story is now Nunavut's—and the world's—first feature film scripted entirely in Inuktitut, and the world's first Inuit-produced film.

The making of a nation, the Canadian critic Elizabeth Waterston has said, is not just about living and working out ways of living together. It is also "the creation of a reflection, an inspiration, a goad and a goal—in art. The artists tell us what they think we are. They help us to hear our own voice, recognize our own shape, laugh at our own follies, rejoice in our own powers. Accepting or rejecting the artists' views, we become more thoroughly ourselves."

Canada has come to have a distinctly Canadian voice. Who can forget Foster Hewitt's familiar "He shoots! He scores!" or Allan McFee's nightly greeting to his audience out in "vacuum land," the elegance of Pierre Nadeau's newscasts over 40 years or the avuncular friendliness of Peter Gzowski? Who cannot be charmed and moved by the stories of Alistair MacLeod, Margaret Atwood, Marie Laberge and Anne Carson?

In 2001, Canada's Janet Cardiff and George Bures Miller were honoured at the Venice Biennale for their multimedia work, *The Paradise Institute*. That award followed closely on the heels of the Millennium Prize, the National Gallery's first international prize in the visual arts awarded to Cardiff for her *Forty-Part Motet*.

More and more, the stories of Canadians have been finding their way onto a larger stage, and increasingly the stage for many great Canadian artists is the world. From the music of our composers to the poetry of our writers, from the sculptures and canvasses of our artists to the gestures of our dancers, from the stories of our filmmakers and the voices of our broadcasters to the bold lines of our architects—Canada is coming to be understood through the creations of its artists.

Yet many of Canada's artists struggle financially. In 1999, the average annual income for someone working in the cultural sector was $27,900, compared with the national average income of $31,800. Since many artists are self-employed—51% in 2001, compared with 16% for the total Canadian work force—earning a living is even more precarious. At $17,300 a year, they earned about 54% of the average Canadian income.

In 2001, an intrepid 23,600 Canadians described themselves as writers, and they were part of a 265,000 strong labour force of artists. In all, however, some 733,000 Canadians work in the cultural sector and the entire impact of this group, measured by its contribution to Canada's Gross Domestic Product, totals more than $33 billion.

In the past half-century, government policies have helped breathe life into this sector, beginning with the 1951 Massey Commission, which recommended the establishment of the National Library and the Canada Council.

Although creativity continues to flourish, government support for the arts declined in the 1990s. Federal, provincial and municipal governments contributed $5.9 billion to cultural activities in 1999–2000. This is about the same amount as in 1992–93,

"There may have to be some visual cues...and if so, I will be able to give these from the raft in the centre of the lake."

R. Murray Schafer, composer

when government spending on the arts reached a peak. In the intervening years, however, spending fell to a low of $5.6 billion, and has only begun to return to previous levels in the last two years.

The Canadian cultural sector, especially film and video production, has made significant inroads in exporting our culture to the rest of the world within the last decade. Between 1996 and 2000, our cultural exports increased by about 44% to reach more than $4.2 billion. But we are also one of the world's greatest importers of cultural products. Between 1996 and 2000, imports of cultural products climbed about 24% to more than $6.4 billion.

Yet, the distribution of our cultural products both within and outside Canada faces obstacles. For example, although they account for fewer than two dozen firms in each of the cultural industries, multinationals captured 51% of film distribution revenues, 88% of music recordings sales, 35% of Canadian book sales and 53% of agency sales by marketers and distributors.

Film

In the film *Atanarjuat*, filmmaker Zacharias Kunuk looks at life in the Arctic barrens of 16th century North Baffin and portrays the great themes—love, jealousy and the struggle for power—so eloquently that he was awarded the prestigious Caméra d'or for best first feature film at the 2001 Cannes Film Festival. Kunuk also won five Genies at Canada's annual Genie Awards, including best picture, director and screenplay.

In the Canadian comedy *Men with Brooms*, a small-town curling team gets together for one last crack at the local bonspiel. Unabashedly Canadian—the Montréal Curling Club threw its first rock in 1807—the film treats its viewers to the great Canadian icons: the beaver, the soaring strains of "*O Canada*," small-town Canadian life, and the rigours of the curling rink.

Remembering the Met "I remember the Metropolitan Theatre in Winnipeg. It's closed now—boarded up and lonely looking. There was also the Odeon with its arching precidium and vaulted dome and there was the Uptown over on Academy. A black ceiling with little pinholes in it; you thought you were under a star-filled sky...and then the velvet curtains drew up and back and the lion roared and the movie began."

Not much is left of Canada's old, glamourous movie houses other than our memories of them. Most of them have been boarded up or turned to other purposes: bowling alleys, community halls, even fast-food emporia.

Today, we are more likely to see a movie in a giant cineplex complete with banks of pinball machines and life-sized figures that fly about beneath soaring ceilings. The theatres themselves are often small and so numerous they are numbered so that we may find our way to them.

Architecture aside, the movies in Canada began officially in 1896 when a group of Ottawans paid 10 cents apiece to view Thomas Edison's newest invention—the Vitascope. Recognizing a business opportunity, storefront shops were soon offering viewers a look at their 'nickelodeons' for—you guessed it—a nickel. The rest, as they say, is history. Throughout the 1930s and 1940s, Canadians were quite mad for the movies. In Edmonton alone, monthly attendance figures were several times greater than the city's population.

In the 1950s, the arrival of television chilled our movie ardour somewhat and, from 1952 to 1964, nearly 600 theatres—one-third of all theatres—shut their doors. In 1980, with the introduction of video, there began another drop in movie attendance, a further 22% by 1992.

Today, with the emergence of the multiplexes, the charm of the movies seems once again to have engaged us after four decades of dropping attendance. From 1991 to 2000, we were back under the marquee purchasing 117.8 million tickets—nearly four times our national population.

Fickle though we may be, movies in Canada seem to have a strong river-current pull. Redolent still with the smell of popcorn and our hope for two hours in another world, they continue to hold a firm place in the Canadian heart.

But the real thrill of these two Canadian movies came at the box office. Within the first weekend of its opening, *Brooms* had grossed $1.1 million in ticket sales and had opened in a record 207 Canadian cinemas. *Atanarjuat*, in its opening weeks, surpassed $1 million.

Although the films did not score with the magnitude of many Hollywood block-busters, their ticket sales and wide distribution make them a refreshing exception to the Canadian rule. Most Canadian feature films achieve little exposure to audiences via the cinema or through home video rentals and sales. In 1998, among Canadian film and video distributors, some 68% of total revenue came from the distribution of foreign productions in Canada.

Nevertheless, the business of making and distributing films in Canada has been booming since at least 1988. In 1998–99 alone, distribution sales of films and videos in Canada, coupled with overseas exports, generated revenues of $2.1 billion, up 23% from the previous year. From 1988 to 1998, revenues of the Canadian independent film, television and video production industry nearly doubled from $533 million to just over $1 billion.

Peter Gzowski. 1937–2002. Illustration by Neville Smith.

Radio and Television

It was during the 1930s, the story goes, when Graham Spry, one of the founders of the Canadian Radio League, had begun to despair of getting any serious attention for publicly-funded radio. When he discovered that Prime Minister R.B. Bennett regularly took a massage at the Chateau Laurier's spa, Spry began arranging what looked like chance meetings with the Prime Minister so that he could press his point while they walked back to Parliament Hill together.

Spry's idea paid off. Bennett was quick to appreciate the usefulness of a government-sponsored radio network. In 1932, Bennett established the Canadian Radio Broad-casting Commission, truly the beginning of government backing for the arts and mass

culture. Four years later, the commission became the Canadian Broadcasting Corporation, with a unique mix of public and private stations.

Today, CBC radio has been described as the nation's 'ribbon of reason,' offering Canadians everywhere a convincing and all-encompassing mirror of our lives. In 2000, fully 10.4% of the time Canadians listen to radio was spent with the CBC. Otherwise, we chose from among Canada's 615 private radio stations, including 456 music, 33 talk-oriented and 126 non-commercial stations. With their superior sound quality, FM stations had reached a 72% share of listeners by the fall of 2000.

Our television shows are popular the world over and more than half the revenue from television programming comes from other countries. In 1997–98, direct exports by producers were $254 million, a fourfold increase over the previous decade.

Here at home, *This Hour Has 22 Minutes*, a satirical TV show produced in Halifax, regularly sent Marg, Princess Warrior, to barge into politicians' offices in Ottawa and ask irreverent questions. The humour—much arising from the East Coast—is a favourite of Canadian viewing audiences. Although comedy and drama were the most popular forms of programming in 2000, accounting for more than 39% of total viewing, Canadians also maintain a healthy appetite for news and public affairs— 32% of total viewing for French-speaking Canadians and 21% for English speakers.

Overall, however, we are watching less television. In 2000, we spent an average of 21.5 hours a week, down 10% since 1984. French-speaking Quebecers are the most avid viewers in Canada—with an average of 24.5 hours a week, whereas Albertans watch the least—about 20 hours a week.

Performing Arts

Evelyn Hart flies effortlessly through the air. Rex Harrington takes a turn, spinning athletically, flawlessly. Josée Chouinard bends her body into an improbably pretzel-like

National Pastimes, 1992.
Work by Jim Logan,
Indian Art Centre,
Indian and Northern
Affairs Canada.

shape. R. Murray Schafer conducts *Music for Wilderness Lake* from a raft in the middle of an Ontario lake. Christopher Plummer gives dramatic credibility to the trials of *King Lear* for a Stratford audience. In Canada, the performing arts seem driven by an eclectic and kinetic energy that respects the history of performance while ever breaking new ground.

Statistics Canada surveys several hundred of Canada's performing arts organizations—625 in 1999. It's interesting to look at the breakdown: 350 are theatre groups, another 160 are music groups, 92 are dance troupes and 23 opera companies. With some 13.3 million people queuing for their performances, these companies generated a full $150 million in 1999.

Theatre appears to be most popular in Quebec, where no fewer than 137 active companies hit the boards—the largest number in Canada.

Music lovers thrive in Canada. Every day, no fewer than 14 concerts are played somewhere across the land. Behind the surefootedness of our performers, however, there are often financial struggles that signal a drop in government funding. A new trend has therefore emerged—a great reliance on volunteers and a shift to private sector funding, which has risen by 60% since the early 1990s.

Merrymaking at Fort Chambly, Quebec, 1929. Work by Franklin Hennessey. National Archives of Canada, C-011218.

Recording

Canadian recording artists are now as familiar in Birmingham and Toulouse as they are in Brampton and Trois-Rivières—Bryan Adams, Robert Charlebois, the Barenaked Ladies, Leonard Cohen, Céline Dion, Nelly Furtado, Diana Krall, Alanis Morissette, Oscar Peterson, Shania Twain, Roch Voisine, and many young up-and-comers. Part of their success stems from a 1971 decision by the Canadian Radio-television and Telecommunications Commission requiring all AM radio stations in Canada to play at least 30% Canadian music during certain times of the day. That bold decision is credited with jump-starting the Canadian music industry.

Between 1991 and 1998, the number of sound-recording companies in Canada increased significantly. The biggest was in British Columbia, where the number almost doubled to 42 companies in 1998. Only in the Prairies did the opposite occur, a drop from 29 companies to 22.

In 1998, record companies reported that net sales of recordings by Canadian artists had risen to $154 million. Just seven years before, sales of records with Canadian content had totalled $58 million.

During the same period, Canadians adopted the compact disc as the preferred recording format. The CD increased its market share from under 44% in 1991 to over 80% in 1998. The latest recording format to gain popularity is the MP3, particularly with listeners who share music files over the Internet. In 2000, some 44% of 'Internet households' reported downloading music from the Net.

The Printed Word

In 1908, Lucy Maud Montgomery's first novel, *Anne of Green Gables* launched a literary career that included seven sequels, the autobiographical *Emily* trilogy, as well as a few novels written for adults. Montgomery's accomplishments were matched by those of other popular writers in Canada, including Stephen Leacock, Anne Hébert, Louis Hémon, Sir Charles G.D. Roberts and Ernest Thompson Seton. Nellie McClung's *Sowing Seeds in Danny* sold 100,000 copies and Margaret Marshall Saunders' *Beautiful Joe*, a novel about a pet dog, sold more than one million.

A second literary renaissance, embodied by the likes of Roch Carrier, Mavis Gallant, Margaret Laurence, Hugh McLennan, Mordecai Richler and Gabrielle Roy seemed to spring to life in the 1950s, and it has continued throughout the century with the work of Margaret Atwood, Arlette Cousture, Alice Munro and Michel Tremblay—to name only a few.

Mordecai Richler.
1931–2001.
Courtesy of
Montreal Gazette.

A Season later.
Gatineau Park, Quebec.
Photo by
J. David Andrews,
Masterfile.

The Paper Poet "I entertain an opinion that our forest trees, either hard or soft wood, but more especially the fir, spruce, or poplar, on account of the fibrous quality of these woods, might be easily reduced by a chafing, and manufactured into paper of the finest kind."

So wrote Nova Scotia's Charles Fenerty on October 26, 1844, in a letter to the *Acadian Recorder*. As a young lumberman, Fenerty had discovered that if he ground freshly-cut wood into pulp, he could squeeze out the moisture and as the fibres adhered to each other, turn them into paper. Local legend has it he got the idea from watching wasps build their paper-like nests. Fenerty's idea would ultimately change the way the printed word was presented.

By the time he had publicized his experiments, others had already patented the process of making paper from wood pulp. He therefore made no money from his discovery. He did, however, gain some recognition for his poetry. "Betula Nigra," an epic he wrote about a majestic black birch on his family's farm, won first prize at the Halifax Exhibition in 1854.

A monarch of the forest shade,
By summer's majesty arrived,
In robes of living green.

Antonine Maillet's *Pélagie-la-Charrette* won the Prix Goncourt in 1979, and sold over a million copies in France alone. In 1992, Michael Ondaatje won both the Governor General's Award for English-language fiction and the Booker Prize for *The English Patient*. In 1995, Carol Shields won the Pulitzer Prize for *The Stone Diaries*.

The sprouting of dozens of small presses during the 1960s paralleled an upsurge in poets, dramatists and novelists seeking outlets for their work. By 1999, Canadian book publishing was a multi-billion dollar industry, employing nearly 9,000 people in 700 firms. Slightly more than half of those firms turned a profit, down from close to two-thirds four years earlier. Among the most successful is Harlequin, the world's largest publisher of romance fiction series. In 2001, the company's annual report listed sales of about 153 million books in 94 international markets.

Our reading habits may be undergoing transformation. In 1998, close to three million Canadians used the Internet at least once to read a newspaper, magazine or book. Between 1986 and 1996, the number of book buyers remained steady, although the average Canadian family spent 23% less on books.

The newspaper and magazine world is also changing shape. Between 1992 and 1998, the number of Canadians who read newspapers at least once a month dropped from 92% to 82%. During the same period, magazine readership declined from 80% to 71%. Between 1991 and 1997, as 1,333 Canadian magazines continued publishing, 400 ceased operating and more than 200 new titles appeared. In 1998, some 28% of Canadians visited a library, although a smaller proportion reported borrowing books than in 1992. One year later, in 1999, Canada became one of the first countries in the world to connect all of its schools and public libraries to the Internet.

Visual Arts

While readers were devouring conventionally romantic novels in the early part of the 1900s, many Canadian artists were putting as much distance as they could between their art and the established conventions of their European predecessors. Banding together as the Group of Seven in 1920, Franklin Carmichael, Lawren Harris, A.Y. Jackson, Franz Johnston, Arthur Lismer, J.E.H. MacDonald and F.H. Varley produced striking wilderness sketches and paintings that were decried by critics of the time as "rough, splashy, meaningless...weird landscapes." Today, their body of work still has popular appeal and is considered as uniquely Canadian as it is imaginative.

Contemporary art in Canada features a complex range of approaches: the multi-media art of N.E. Thing Co.; Michael Snow's conceptual work; the body art of Geneviève Cadieux and Mr. Peanut (Vincent Trasov), who ran for mayor of Vancouver dressed as a peanut; the environmental art of the Montréal architect and artist Melvin Charney; the 'mail-art activity' of Anna Banana; the collages of Jeff Wall; the installation art of Edward Poitras, one of many distinguished First Nations artists; and many more.

Only a year after professional photography began in Canada in 1840, a Mrs. Fletcher of Montréal set up her commercial studio and became the first woman photographer in the country. Photography was important for immigrant recruitment to the West. It was also a source of news during both World Wars. The works of Malak and Yousuf Karsh are familiar to many Canadians, and through them and others such as Roloff Beny, John de Visser and Evergon, Canadian photography has earned a high reputation internationally.

"When I hesitate, I do not paint. When I paint, I do not hesitate."

Jean-Paul Riopelle, *Riopelle: Œuvres vives*, 1993.

Isabel Jordan, 1947.
Work by Alma Duncan,
National Archives
of Canada,
C-149239.

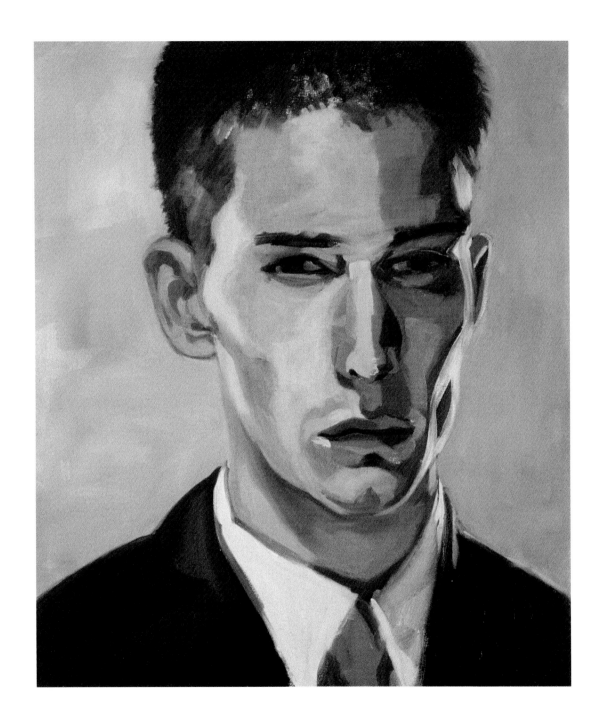

Pretty boy, 2001.

Work by Janet Werner,

Ottawa Art Gallery.

In 2001, more than 27,000 Canadians identified themselves as painters, sculptors, artisans, craftpersons, or photographers—a number virtually unchanged from a decade earlier.

Sports and Leisure

Sports continue to awaken our competitive spirits and we have always had our sports heroes—rower Ned Hanlan and strongman Louis Cyr in the 19th century, and more recently hockey great Wayne Gretzky, skater Catriona Le May Doan and car racers Gilles and Jacques Villeneuve.

Among all leisure activities, hockey seems to move Canadians in a way that no other sport can. When the former Montréal Canadiens star Maurice 'Rocket' Richard died in 2000, Roch Carrier—a devoted fan and author of a recent book on the Rocket— wrote: "In our memories the Rocket will never stop skating, never stop scoring goals. We will hear, 'Maurice Rocket Richard shoots—he scores!' till the end of our lives."

In February 2002, close to six million Canadians watched the final Olympic women's hockey match in Salt Lake City, Utah and the cheers were deafening as Canada won 3–2 over the United States, bringing home our first gold medal ever in this sport. A few days later, the cheers went up again as the men's hockey team also won gold— providing support for writer Joey Slinger's contention that "the field of our dreams is flooded and frozen and has a net at either end." Altogether, Canada collected 17 medals, the best Olympic result since first competing in 1924.

Hockey's roots can be traced back to lacrosse, British rugby and a game played with a makeshift puck in Montréal in 1875. We can track the origins of other Canadian sports to a variety of sources. Curling first came to Canada from Scotland and native Canadians are credited with canoeing, lacrosse, snowshoeing and tobogganing. Basketball was invented by a Canadian, James Naismith.

We may love to watch high-performance athletes and hockey players, but golf is the sport of choice for most Canadians. In 1998, a new leisure trend emerged when golf supplanted hockey as the sport most adults reported playing. More than 1.8 million golfers hit the links that year, compared with the 1.5 million who strapped on hockey skates. The golf trend underscores ongoing changes in our society; as the overall population ages, popular tastes and cultural interests are shifting.

Much of the work that goes into maintaining amateur sport falls on the shoulders of volunteers. Between 1992 and 1998, twice as many of us decided that coaching amateur sport was a worthwhile activity, the numbers rising from an estimated 840,000 Canadians to 1.7 million. The number of referees, officials and umpires almost doubled during the same period, mushrooming from an estimated 550,000 to almost 940,000.

Many of us still enjoy quieter pastimes, such as gardening. In 1998, about 12% of us reported that we painted or sculpted. At the same time, about 29% of us take pleasure in crafts—including woodcarving, weaving, and pottery—and about 8% spend time engaged in artistic photography.

"The winters of my childhood were long, long seasons. We lived in three places—the school, the church and the skating-rink—but our real life was on the skating-rink."

Roch Carrier,
The Hockey Sweater, 1979

119

We did it!
Women's Olympic
Hockey Team, 2002.
Canadian Press
(Kevork Djansezian).

Canada's Family Album "History for me is a whole steamer trunk full of stories," the novelist Jack Hodgins once said. But where is that trunk? We haven't lost the secrets of who we are, or forgotten what we once were. They still exist in Canada's treasure chest of memory—a vast stainless steel and glass building designed to last at least 500 years—the new National Archives Gatineau Preservation Centre in Gatineau, Quebec.

Rare old videotapes of the comedians Johnny Wayne and Frank Shuster. The personal diaries of Prime Minister Mackenzie King. Unpublished poetry by Archibald Lampman. Decrypted messages sent by enemy spies during the Second World War. The papers of the great Quebec actor and playwright Gratien Gélinas. Here are so many pages from Canada's 'family album,' what National Archivist Ian Wilson has described as "writing and recollection, in image and anecdote, in court testimony and tall tale."

Since 1872, the National Archives has been preserving "the gift of one generation to another," as Sir Arthur Doughty, Dominion Archivist from 1904 to 1935, called its holdings. "The extent of our care of them marks the extent of our civilization."

Karst family, 1945.
Courtesy of Roz Phillips.

To be keepers of all this history and memory, Canada's archivists face the daunting task of sifting through billions of government and private sector records, stories and pieces of news to decide the 1% that is 'archival' and worthy of the 'national memory.' To this end, they maintain world-class labs where they repair and treat fragile documents and run seven huge centres across the country where dormant government records are stored. All of this so that researchers and interested Canadians may find the "proverbial needle in a very, very large haystack."

Over time, the results of this labour have been impressive. Today, the Archives holds some 2.3 million maps and architectural plans, Canada's most valuable stamp collection, 341,000 hours of film, video and sound recordings, and well over 20 million photographs. If all its holdings were piled high, they would extend 145 kilometres into the air. For Canadians, it would appear that our past remains very much alive and secure, not only in our memory but in our national 'family album' as well.

The Karst Family

Tree line,
Gatineau, Quebec.
Photo by
Mary F. Hawkins.

I was born in 1908 on a farm in Elgin County, Ontario.

The nearest town was Iona Station. Population: 19.

There were two things that made me unhappy about my life on a farm. There was the physical toll to which I had a not exceptional aversion and there was the low pecuniary return. You worked very hard for very little.

When it came time to choose, I was very happy to pursue life as an academic, a writer and a teacher.

To young people today, I would say this: "There's only one place you should seek to be and that is at the top of your class."

John Kenneth Galbraith, economist

Peewee power,

Burlington, Ontario.

Photo by John de Visser.

THE ECONOMY

"Money," said the Canadian-born economist John Kenneth Galbraith, "ranks with love as man's greatest source of joy. And with death as his greatest source of anxiety." The editor of the lively *Calgary Eye Opener*, Bob Edwards, once lamented that "if money talks, all it ever said to me was good-bye." In the same spirit, the thrill of a roll of the dice or a turn at blackjack is not unknown in Canada—in 2001, Canadians bet a not insignificant $10.7 billion. Perhaps it's not accidental that our very first paper money, the first in North America, was written on the back of playing cards in New France in 1685.

In keeping with a national penchant for saving over the years, we have supported a large number of savings banks. Canadian historian William Kilbourn records the astonishment of a visitor to pioneer Saskatchewan on seeing "a sod hut in the middle of the prairie open for business under a large Canadian Bank of Commerce sign." And if a nice crisp $4 bill from Nova Scotia's Commercial Bank of Windsor turns up under the mattress, the Bank of Canada will still redeem it for $4—even though this tiny Nova Scotia bank hasn't been around for 100 years. On the other hand, it's probably worth many multiples of this to a collector.

Private banks—from the phantom Agricultural Bank in Montréal to the short-lived Zimmerman Bank of Elgin, Canada West—issued nearly all our paper money until 1935, when the newly created Bank of Canada began to gradually phase out private bank notes as it took on the job exclusively.

Although winning a lottery or discovering a hoard of money is a dream for many, most Canadians build wealth through working and saving. In 2001, Canada's wealth reached a total of $3.5 trillion; if one were to divide that among all of us, we'd each be worth an average of about $112,800. In 1999 alone, we placed $27.8 billion in registered retirement savings plans (RRSPs), bringing the total of all private pension assets to well over a trillion dollars. On the other hand, our predilection for saving is dwindling somewhat. In 2001, personal savings came to $23.4 billion, a far cry from the $62.9 billion banked in 1992.

It is also possible to calculate the net worth—the assets minus the debts—of what economists call the 'median family,' that is, the family that falls exactly halfway down the list of all 12.2 million Canadian families. By this measure, Canada's median family had a net worth of $81,000 in 1999.

However, wealth in Canada is not spread evenly. In 1999, the richest 10% of families possessed 53% of total wealth. At the other end of the scale, the poorest 10% of families had a negative net worth; debts were greater than assets. Education makes some of the difference. In 1999, someone with a master's degree had a median net worth almost three times higher than that of a person with a high-school diploma.

Not surprisingly, the home is the single most important asset for Canadian families, representing 32% of all the assets held in 1999. Canadians are home lovers. To own one's home is an oft-cited Canadian dream, a "special space, standing apart from the practical world," as Canadian architect Witold Rybczynski has noted. Next in importance are private pension assets—largely employer pension plans, RRSPs and registered retirement investment funds (RRIFs)—which account for 29% of all assets.

"You miss 100% of the shots you don't take."

Wayne Gretzky

Canada Today

A young person enters the Canadian work force in 2002. What are his or her chances of finding a job and enjoying a comfortable, healthy life? As it turns out, they are not tied to winning a lottery. Instead, they are very much tied to the level of education and job experience—what economists call human capital. Quite simply, the more educated a young person is, the better the chance of finding the security of a well-paying job.

The economic numbers tell a further compelling story. Canada is the world's ninth largest economy and boasts one of the highest levels of income and wealth. It now takes 13 digits to measure the Canadian economy: in 2001, the gross domestic product (GDP)—the total of all goods and services produced within Canadian borders—reached the $1 trillion mark.

And what of inflation? From 1973 to 1981, inflation was in the double digits, fuelled as it was by rising oil prices. Then, it fell sharply to just 5%. Over the last decade, it has remained well under that; in 2001, it was 2.6%.

Like economies throughout the world, the Canadian economy suffered a significant slowdown in 2001. The terrorist attacks of September 11 amplified the trend, rocking financial and commodity markets and showing just how vulnerable the global economy is to such occurrences. The quick return to growth was testimony to its resilience and flexibility, which played itself out in a country-wide shopping spree for new homes, furniture and many other consumer goods. Consumer spending accounted for 57% of our GDP in 2001, not too far off from the 61% of GDP of 40 years earlier.

In fact, Canada's GDP gain of 1.5% ranked as one of the strongest international showings in 2001. By comparison, the United States' output grew 1.2%, whereas Japan's economy shrank by 0.5%, the culmination of a decade of poor performance. Meanwhile, Germany, once the economic engine of Europe, continued to lag behind.

In Canada, the phenomenal growth of the high-tech industry came to a virtual standstill as it lost the equivalent of $10 billion. Manufacturers of computers, telecommunication equipment and fibre-optic cable were especially hard hit. For those providing services in computer design, software, and telecommunications, the growth remained quite strong, but slowed.

The economic slowdown of 2001 also cost other industries: natural resources industries lost almost $7 billion; the mining and lumber industries suffered considerably; and Canada's farmers experienced the largest loss as their harvests dropped 18%, partly the result of the worst drought since 1988. In the last decade, more than 100,000 farm workers—over 30% of all the people who worked at farming—left the agricultural sector.

Corporate Office,

1976.

Work by Lynne Cohen.

The Bombardier Story On a snowy winter night in 1934, Joseph-Armand Bombardier was called home from his garage in Valcourt, Quebec, to find his two-year-old son Yvon gravely ill with appendicitis. Since Quebec's back roads were blanketed in heavy snow, it was impossible for Bombardier to reach the nearest hospital in Sherbrooke, some 50 kilometres away, and sadly, young Yvon died.

For Bombardier, the tragedy was especially difficult since he had been puzzling the concept of a machine that could travel the snow since he was a teenager.

In fact, Bombardier had concocted his first machine as a 15-year-old, using an old sleigh, a propeller and the motor from a Model T Ford. The story goes that he and his brother rode this noisy machine a kilometre over the town's main street, frightening horses and towns-people into the bargain.

As biographer Roger Lacasse tells it, "…their father was furious. 'Do you want to kill yourselves?' he shouted at the top of his lungs—and ordered them to dismantle the vehicle immediately."

Bombardier did finally invent Canada's first motorized snow vehicle. In June 1937, he received his first patent and soon after, production of his 'auto-neige' began.

The story evolved as Bombardier refined his invention and, in 1959, he unveiled a new, lightweight snowmobile. He called it the Ski-Dog, but when the literature was printed, a typographical error changed the name to Ski-Doo and it stuck. An instant hit. A 1963 issue of *Imperial Oil Review* called it a "kind of scooter mounted on toy tracks and which growls like a runaway dishwasher."

Bombardier's company has gone on to sell more than two million snowmobiles worldwide and to become one of the world's major suppliers not only of the Ski-Doo, but of airplanes, trains, military vehicles, public transit systems and recreational watercraft.

Courtesy of Canada Post.

Canada's decline in commercial fishing has been headline news, but despite the setbacks, moratoriums and controls on many species, fishing is still important to hundreds of coastal communities and to even a few inland towns. Fishing communities and fishing companies have adapted, mainly by expanding into shellfish and other types of aquaculture. In 2000, the value of landed catches of shellfish increased by 27%.

Trade

Trade has always been important to Canada—"the vital question upon which patriotism, common defence and everything else will depend," Sir William Van Horne wrote in 1914.

Much has been written on the vagaries of our trading, and much more is no doubt yet to come. What we do know is that Canada is a small population in a large land and from that land has come a wealth of water and wood and mineral treasure—these natural endowments have helped to shape the way we do business with the world. Early Europeans were first attracted to Canada's abundance of fish off Newfoundland's shore and, during the 1800s, the European penchant for fur led to the exploration of Canada's West. In the early years, we traded largely with the British, selling our lumber for their ship-building industry, wheat and, of course, beaver pelts. In return, they sent us textiles and fine china and railroad cars.

With the onset of the Second World War, however, there was a shift in our trade away from the United Kingdom and toward the United States, which was now in a more financially robust position to buy our goods. By 1946, a full 45% of our exports were from our mines, oceans, forests and farms; close to 40% were destined to the United States.

Fundamentally, our trade today comprises that at which we excel. We are very good at making cars and airplanes, snowmobiles and trains, not to mention

Confederation Bridge.

Photo by John Sylvester.

telecommunications equipment. While we still trade in wheat, lumber, pulp and paper, minerals and now even diamonds, by 2000, natural resources represented less than 40% of our exports. In fact, Canada's single most important trade commodity today is the automobile, and, of course, auto parts. The next two largest categories include 'machinery and equipment' and industrial goods. This includes everything from aircraft to portable cassette players. But trade is a multi-variegated phenomenon and one of Canada's indefatigable ambassadors in this regard is maple syrup: our prime consumers, none other than the Americans, buy 80% of this Canadian elixir. The Americans, in turn, produce a similarly wide rainbow of consumer and capital goods.

During the last 50 years, we have typically had an overall trade deficit, which means we spend more on imports than we earn on our exports. In 2001, however, we registered a trade surplus for only the sixth time since 1950, exporting nearly $471 billion in goods and services while importing $416 billion. Our current-account surplus rose to $30 billion in 2001, breaking the previous year's record by $2.3 billion. This marked the third straight surplus and the longest string of surpluses since the 1940s.

That would have made George Hees happy. As Canada's Minister of Trade and Commerce from 1960 to 1963, he was wont to say that he'd "stand on his head in Times Square if it would sell Canadian." When Hees took office, the United States was already our most important trading partner. Further, as trade barriers have lowered over the years, our exports to the United States have soared 300%. At a joint session of Parliament in 1995, U.S. President Bill Clinton neatly summed up the significance of this calling it the "essential pillar in the architecture of both our economies."

In 2001, some 85% of Canadian exports were destined to the United States. These numbers do not include other forms of economic integration, such as workers moving between the two countries, business-to-business e-commerce, and Internet shopping.

October, 1993, Montréal.

Photo by Barbara Meneley.

Europe and Japan are important trading partners as well, and sources of foreign investment. Canada has also signed bilateral free trade agreements with Chile, Costa Rica and Israel, as we invest more in developing economies.

Fresh Thought

In 2000, a science writer set out across Canada to find out what really lay at the heart of the new knowledge-based economy. At the end of his visit to Canada's new and upcoming high-tech companies, William Atkinson wrote *Prototype*, concluding that the key to today's economy is to "harness the most renewable and widely available of all our resources—fresh thought."

Everywhere, the pace of change seems to have quickened, the consequence of this fresh thinking and technological innovation. In 1994, a pizza chain accepted its first order through the Internet for a pizza—pepperoni and mushroom, no less—just three years after the World Wide Web was launched. The potential impact of the Internet and the World Wide Web on communications has been so great that even the 'bricks and mortar' firms stepped up their investments in technology to keep up with their online competitors.

Two recent phenomena changed the face of Canada's high-tech sector: the so-called Y2K (Year 2000) bug and the rise of the 'dot.coms.' Throughout 1999, computer owners around the world seemed to suffer a case of millennial angst as they antici- pated the effect of the Y2K bug, a computer glitch that would have some computer programs confusing January 1, 2000 with January 1, 1900.

Anticipating chaos, Canadian businesses, governments and individuals overhauled and upgraded a wide range of computer and information systems. The collective force of this renovation helped push the economy to its best performance in a generation. The demand was fuel to the financial markets and centred on stocks and new offerings of companies catering to the Internet. Generally, their web addresses ended in '.com'—for 'commercial'—and the popularity of these dot.coms helped create an enormous stock-market bubble.

There also seemed to be a sense of euphoria about the new millennium. Many believed that new models of business growth and profitability were replacing the old rules of the business cycle. Indeed, iconic firms such as Eaton's and Enron fell prey to market forces, while companies that did not even exist a decade ago attracted huge investments.

The bubble was to burst, however. It began in March 2000 with the crash of many high-tech stocks included in the NASDAQ index (National Association of Securities Dealers Automated Quotations), and by August 2000, the decline had spread to the Toronto Stock Exchange (TSE). By August 2001, the TSE Index had tumbled 34%.

Stock Markets

In Canada, stocks were first traded at the Exchange Coffee House in Montréal in 1832. Between 1945 and 1998, over 39 billion shares changed hands through the Montréal Stock Exchange.

The most notable stock market crash was soon followed by the Great Depression. In the summer of 1929, industrial stock prices in Canada had soared; by September, they were triple the level of early 1927. Just two months later, they had fallen 33% and kept sliding for another four years. Despite booms and busts, stocks have been a source of wealth for investors over the long term. A sum of $1,000 invested in the broad Canadian stock market index in 1924 would be worth almost $2 million today.

Today, Canada's stock market acts as a gauge of our economic optimism and the health of our economy. For example, with the slowdown in 2001, foreign investors

"$\Delta N = n \Delta Y$

where $0 < n < 1$

is the marginal

propensity to spend

out of national

income."

Lipsey, Purvis, Sparks, Steiner
Economics, 4th edition, 1982

Who Has Seen The Wind? Not far from W.O. Mitchell country, in Pincher Creek, Alberta, prairie winds have achieved something other than literary coin: they are being harvested to generate the same electrical power we might get from water, gas or coal.

The harvesters stand some 50 meters high and bear only a passing similarity to windmills with their giant blades and rotors the size of airplane wings.

Together, they turn the prevailing prairie westerlies into 40,000 kilowatts an hour of usable electricity, part of the 299 million kilowatt hours of power produced annually by wind turbines across Canada. That's enough to keep all the homes of a mid-sized Canadian city humming for six months of the year.

Wind power is also pollution-free and that was fair cause for Calgary to switch its train system to power supplied by the spinning Pincher Creek turbines. The switchover, which took place in 2001, means that 187,000 people in Calgary are ferried by Calgary Transit's C-Train to and from work every day on wind power. (The concept to power the C-Train by wind is the proud idea of Vision Quest Windelectric Inc. of Pincher Creek.)

The first public transit system in North America to be powered by wind, Calgary Transit estimates it would take the equivalent of 50,000 tonnes of coal to produce the annual power the railway needs, not to mention the 26,000 tonnes of carbon dioxide emissions that would ensue.

Wind power in Canada has been around for some time, but it was only in 1987 that the first wind 'farm' appeared at remote Cambridge Bay on Victoria Island in the Canadian Archipelago.

The "unfailing visitation of wind" was how W.O. Mitchell described it in the opening lines of his 1947 novel *Who has Seen the Wind*. For the wind farms of Canada that unfailing quality promises well, not only as a source of power, but as a future means of keeping our air fresh and our winds free of pollution.

A crossing,

Jasper National Park,

Alberta.

Courtesy of Via Rail

Canada.

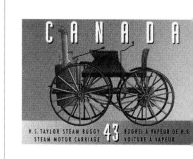

Full Steam Ahead A local newspaper praised it as "the neatest thing of the kind yet invented." Its maker—Henry Seth Taylor—boasted that it would challenge "any trotting horse."

In 1867, at a country fair in what is now Stanstead, Quebec, Canada's first self-propelled automobile chugged into motion. Though it was built long after the world's first car in 1769, Taylor's conveyance was the first recorded steam buggy built in Canada.

Canada's automotive industry did not really begin until the establishment of the Ford Motor Company of Canada, Ltd. in 1904. By 1913, just as the American industrialist Henry Ford was beginning his mass production assembly lines, more than 29,000 cars were motoring on Canada's roads. Ten years later, Canada was a close second to the United States as the largest vehicle producer and major exporter of automobiles and auto parts.

In 1927, the *Canada Year Book* reported, rather primly, that: "Like many other inventions, the motor car commenced as a toy, then became a luxury of the rich, while it now ranks as a necessity to those in moderate circumstances and it may even become a necessity of life to the masses."

It did. As Canadians struggled through the Great Depression, they nonetheless registered more than a million cars annually. In a population of roughly 10 million, that meant one car for every 10 Canadians. In the early 1950s, as shopping malls mushroomed across the land, more than two million cars were registered and some 50% of Canadian homes had at least one parked in the driveway.

By 1965, the year of the Canada–U.S. Autopact, more than five million passenger vehicles were licensed, the equivalent of almost one car for every four Canadians.

By 1990, the number of cars on Canadian roads had more than doubled to over 12 million. In 2000, more than 136,500 people were employed in motor vehicle and motor vehicle parts manufacturing in Ontario alone.

Today, the average Canadian travels about 15,440 kilometres a year in a car, a van or a small truck. In Taylor's day, cars had no odometers and no statistics were kept, but historians tell us that, at best, drivers may have averaged about 160 kilometres a year.

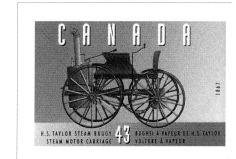

CANADA

H.S. TAYLOR STEAM BUGGY 43 BOGHEI À VAPEUR DE H.S. TAYLOR
STEAM MOTOR CARRIAGE   VOITURE À VAPEUR

abandoned Canadian stock markets; foreign investment there plunged from $35 billion in 2000 to just $5 billion in 2001. At the same time, foreign investors supplied $34 billion to the thriving bond market. Canadian companies acted swiftly to lock in relatively low interest rates in 2001 and increased new bond issues to $58 billion, up from $12 billion the year before. They also used bond issues to reduce their reliance on short-term loans.

Given a lacklustre stock market at home, Canadian investors remained far more interested in accumulating foreign stocks than in buying foreign bonds. In 2001, Canadian portfolio investors bought $36 billion of stock versus nearly nothing in bonds.

Spend, Spend

Despite the faltering economy, Canadian families actually found themselves with more take-home pay in 2001. Thus, the actual cash we had to spend grew by 2.4%, albeit a little less than what we had in 2000.

This was the result partly of one of the largest tax breaks that the government has provided Canadians since 1978, and partly of wage settlements that bespeak a relatively tight labour market. Workers in the private sector, for instance, negotiated wage increases averaging 2.4% in 2000 and an even more robust 2.9% in 2001.

With "For Sale" signs springing up on the nation's lawns and roadways and with bargain basement mortgages for sale at the banks, Canadians began shopping for houses, which led to a very vibrant housing market. In fact, along with consumer spending, the purchase of a home took centre stage for our economic growth in 2001.

Big purchases aside, the higher incomes of 2001 allowed Canadian consumers to spend while continuing to save at a rate of 4.6%. In fact, our ability to keep spending without dipping into savings or running up debt stands in marked contrast with the

United States, even if we are not the savers we once were. For the most part, per capita spending has been increasing steadily for more than 20 years in Canada, whereas savings rates have been on the decline.

However, our purchasing patterns have shifted slightly. Our medical and health spending grew last year, partly the result of new drugs targeted to an aging population. We also continue our love affair with the automobile; in 2001, there was even something of a flurry of purchases at the end of the year when interest rates dropped.

Jobs

In the early 1900s, Alfred Fuller, a 21-year-old Nova Scotian, had already been fired from three jobs when he decided to begin the Fuller Brush Company in his sister's basement in Boston. It would soon become a North American success story. By the 1950s, some 1,200 'Fuller Brush men' set out each day, ringing doorbells to sell their wares across Canada. Today, the idea of selling brushes—or vacuum cleaners, encyclopaedias or anything else, for that matter—door-to-door has given way to selling them at the mall, on the shopping channel, or over the Internet.

Many of the jobs held by our parents and our grandparents have simply disappeared. Job advertisements for blacksmiths, typesetters and railway firemen are long gone from the help-wanted sections. In fact, the number one occupation today in Canada for men is trucking while for women it's clerking.

These days, 76% of Canadians in the labour force work in services, a sector that has generally been growing faster than others. Of these workers, about 20% work in business services, finance and administration areas.

Whether it's the fierce urge for independence or for a combination of social or economic reasons, 15% of Canadian workers—2.3 million—work for themselves. Of these self-employed workers, 33% are women. The surge of women into the paid

"I felt no special sense of vocation. If God had created me to become a chemist, he had neglected to inform me of the fact."

John Polanyi,
1986 Nobel Prize in chemistry

Regina street corner,
Saskatchewan.
Photo by Yves Beaulieu,
ALT-6.

work force began during the Second World War, continued in earnest in the 1960s, and has continued more or less unabated ever since. Today, some 21% of husband–wife families have a single earner compared with 44% in 1975.

In 2001, Canada's labour force was more than 16 million strong. It comprised 66% of the working age population. Our unemployment rate was just over 7% compared with 11% in the early 1990s. Nonetheless, there is a phenomenon that Canadian economist Judith Maxwell has described as young workers looking for 'pieces of work' rather than jobs, because permanent jobs have grown slowly.

Although the job market since 1999 seems to have become tougher for those with more than a bachelor's degree (the jobless rate for university graduates rose for the first time in five years from 3.9% to 4.6%), there is still a close link between higher education and better jobs. The change may well reflect the downturn in technology industries, which employ a higher proportion of highly educated people than do other industries. But the persistence of this trend over three years, including two boom years in technology, suggests that additional but not yet understood factors may be at work. The drop in the unemployment rate has been concentrated among men over 24 years of age, especially those between 25- and 44-years-old and those over 64.

The Public Purse

In the mid-1950s, C.D. Howe, then Minister of Trade and Commerce quipped, somewhat facetiously, that "there is nothing more permanent than a temporary government building, unless it's a temporary tax." Although Canada's first income tax, in 1917, had been intended as a short-term measure to pay our military bills from World War I, it remains as much a fact of life today as temporary government buildings. In 2001, federal and provincial governments collected more than $187 billion in income taxes, which came to more than 45% of government revenues. In 1917, the first year of modern 'taxation', revenue from personal income tax came to $8 million.

Like families and individuals, federal, provincial and local governments also receive revenues from various sources, such as personal and corporate income tax, property taxes, custom duties and user fees.

On the other side of the equation lie the expenditures. For the federal government, and many of the provincial governments, deficit spending was standard practice from the 1970s until well into the 1990s. Between 1971 and 2001, the federal government debt therefore mushroomed from $18.6 billion to $545 billion, or from the equivalent of about $900 for each man, woman and child, up to nearly $18,000 per person. Most of this money is owed to citizens who hold Canada Savings Bonds, treasury bills and other government securities. The remainder is owed to foreign lenders.

Between 1996 and 2001, there was a sharp shift in our fiscal management. In fact, we have had five years of budgetary surpluses since 1996, including $34 billion in 2000 and $26 billion in 2001. These surpluses have helped reduce our debt and have reinforced in the process what economists call the 'virtuous circle' by lowering payments needed to service the debt.

Since deficits have swung now to surpluses—at least for the last five years— the ratio of government debt to the GDP has also shrunk, from 71% in 1995 to just a little over 50% in 2001. Once the debt is reduced, we pay less interest through various kinds of taxes. In 2001, the interest bill for Canada's national debt came to about $41 billion or about $1,335 for every one of us, children included.

The Shape of a Gesture,

1978.

Work by Sorel Cohen.

Cold Carats Great, wide expanses of snow and ice. Low knobs of rock and the occasional ridge of gravel. Sketchy boreal forests. Lake after lake after lake. Muskox, caribou and the odd loping polar bear. Silence.

Such a description of the North might have been blessed by geographer and poet alike up until 1991, when pieces of Canada's North quite literally vaulted into the fine drawing rooms of the world.

What took them there was the discovery of 81 smallish gems recovered from deep beneath icy Point Lake in the heart of the Northwest Territories.

Some nine million carats later, Canada is the world's fourth largest diamond producer, after Botswana, Russia and Namibia.

In 2001 alone, Canada produced 3.7 million carats valued at some $800 million. All come from a single mine—Ekati—situated at Lac de Gras, some 380 kilometres north of Yellowknife. Plans for two more mines at Diavik and Snap Lake are underway and annual diamond production in Canada is expected to yield a sparkling $1.2 billion by 2010.

The Ekati Mine alone has added nearly 20% to the Northwest Territories' gross domestic product and created more than 2,200 jobs. Grist for the economy. Ancient Arctic ice for sale.

Northern lights,

Sudbury, Ontario.

Photo by Mike Grandmaison.

I was born in 1957 in a sod house on Jens Munk Island.

I never went past Grade 8 because I didn't want to leave home for a school 400 miles away. Everyone tells me that Atanarjuat touches on the universal themes. But I never read Shakespeare and I never read the Greek tragedies.

I just listened to the stories our elders told us as we were growing up.

In 1981, I got hold of a movie camera and I never looked back.

My philosophy was this: if they could do it, I probably could do it too. And I did.

Zacharias Kunuk, movie director

Inuit elders,

Arctic Bay, Nunavut.

Photo by Mike Beedell.

CANADA IN THE WORLD

In 1971, a young cabinet minister named Jean Chrétien travelled to the Soviet Union and donated 10 muskox as a gift of friendship to the Soviet people. Little did he realize at the time that these woolly mammals would grow to become a robust herd of 2,500 roaming Russia's far north. Simple acts of diplomacy such as this one help shape Canada's place in the world, as do our activities in fields as varied as peace-keeping, science and technology, literature and the fine arts, and sports.

Since the first peacekeeping force was created in response to the 1956 Suez Crisis, Canadians have been involved in nearly every peacekeeping initiative undertaken by the United Nations (UN), serving in such places as Kashmir, Cyprus, the Middle East, Haiti and Africa. In 1992, Canadian Major-General Lewis MacKenzie headed the UN Protection Force in Yugoslavia; in 2001, Canadian peacekeepers were dispatched to Macedonia at the request of the North Atlantic Treaty Organization.

Travelling at more than 27,000 kilometres per hour, the International Space Station is another symbol of international diplomacy, as Canadians collaborate on the largest scientific endeavour in history. Since Marc Garneau's first mission in 1984, Canadians have taken part in 11 space missions, adventures each, including the first space walk by a Canadian in 2001, by astronaut Chris Hadfield.

"I write to trick reality into revealing itself," poet and novelist George Bowering once said, and increasingly the new reality being honoured around the world is Canadian. In 2001, Alistair MacLeod's IMPAC Dublin Literary Award for *No Great Mischief* placed him securely in the pantheon of international writing stars. The year before, Margaret Atwood was the second Canadian to win the Booker Prize for her novel *The Blind Assassin* (Michael Ondaatje won in 1992 for *The English Patient*), and in 2002, Anne Carson became the first woman and first Canadian ever to win the T.S. Eliot Prize, for her poetic, *The Beauty of the Husband*.

Canadians are among the wealthiest citizens of the world, with an average income of US$28,000 in 2000—there are only six other countries where average incomes are greater. The citizens of Luxembourg earned the most, with US$45,000 each, while Americans averaged US$36,000. Few other people share in this sort of wealth. In 1999, the average individual income around the world was below US$7,000, and for Sierra Leoneans—among the poorest people on earth—it was less than US$450.

From 1994 to 2000, the UN rated Canada as the best nation on the planet in terms of health, education, literacy, employment and income; in 2001, Canada ranked third, just behind Norway and Australia.

Health

Only since the 1950s have humans begun to outlive Amazon parrots and elephants, both of which can survive to almost 80 years of age. In 1920, faced with the rigours and challenges of daily life, Canadian citizens could expect to live an average of only 59 years; by the 1950s, our average life expectancy had reached 69 years. Today, it has risen to nearly 79 years.

Today, Canadians on average live longer than anyone except the citizens of Japan, Australia, Sweden, Iceland, Switzerland and Hong Kong. The people of Japan live the longest, enjoying an average life span of some 80 years. Not everyone is as fortunate. In 1999, average life expectancy around the world was less than 67 years, and in the least developed countries, life expectancy was 50 years.

In 1998, each Canadian spent more than US$2,300 on health care, compared with more than US$4,000 spent by each American—the most of any country in the world. Canadian governments spent 6.6% of Canada's gross domestic product (GDP) on health care. Compare that with 7.0% in Iceland and Sweden, 7.7% in Switzerland, and 7.9% in Germany and Belgium.

During the 1980s and 1990s, human immunovirus (HIV) and acquired immune deficiency syndrome (AIDS) emerged as a worldwide health concern. In 2001, an

"Being conscious of how well or poorly we ourselves walk enables us to see the other walking in his way."

John Ralston Saul,
On Equilibrium, 2001

A Flying Jeep For many pilots, it's been their flying half-ton truck and during the Korean War, it was called the flying jeep. Northern Canadians knew it simply as their lifeline—the De Havilland Canada Beaver.

For them, the unmuffled roar of a bush plane has been one of the most welcome sounds in Canada's North. Swooping in with mail, food, fuel and a thousand other necessities, then leaving with a sick child to be taken to hospital, or perhaps bringing in the entire staff of a circuit court, bush planes have been linking remote communities since northern flights began in the mid-1920s.

Canadian bush pilots were heroes—portrayed in children's books about the 1920s and 30s like *Renfrew Flies Again* and *Dick Kent and the Malemute Mail*—and Canadian engineers were equally heroic in their efforts to design a rugged single-engined machine that could handle rough landing conditions in Canada's Far North. The first all-Canadian bush plane, Bob Noorduyn's Norseman, sold more than 900 craft after it began flying in 1935.

But nothing could match the Beaver. Shortly after the Second World War, a team of designers at the De Havilland Canada aircraft company in Toronto produced a prototype of the first successful all-metal, Canadian-designed bush plane. The DHC-2 Beaver took off on August 16, 1947 and, after a production run of almost 1,700 planes, has flown into aviation history books as the toughest, hardest-working aircraft ever produced in Canada.

In 1987, the Engineering Centennial Board recognized the Beaver as one of Canada's 10 most outstanding engineering feats of the past century, along with the CPR transcontinental railway and the St. Lawrence Seaway.

Eventually the remarkable Beaver was superseded by the Super Beaver, De Havilland Canada's more powerful DHC-3 Otter. But even today some 400 Beavers are still in service, reconditioned, reconfigured and working just as hard as ever.

There has always been a certain drama to the Beaver—even to this day—as the Welsh writer Jan Morris discovered on a trip to Yellowknife. Seeing a motionless light in the sky at dusk, she thought it might have been Jupiter.

"Silently it hung there against the darkening sky, and only very slowly, majestically indeed, did it resolve itself into the form of a single small float-plane, bearing down on Yellowknife out of the north. Its light seemed so defiantly bright, the aircraft itself was so small, that when at last it landed with plumes of spray on the surface of the lake, I thought it a truly heroic image of Canada's northern adventure."

Ottawa by night.

Photo by Malak.

estimated 55,000 Canadians were infected with HIV/AIDS—about 0.3% of the population aged 15 to 49. This was the average rate of infection for the most developed nations and about half that of the United States.

The situation elsewhere, however, is much worse. In 2001, Sub-Saharan Africa's average rate of infection was nearly 30 times higher than that of Canada, with 9% of the region's adult population infected with HIV or AIDS.

Education

Nearly every Canadian can read, write and understand a short simple sentence, but in 1998, about 17% had difficulty in understanding forms, charts, timetables and maps. Interestingly, in 1901, the Census of Canada also found that 17% of Canadians could not read or write, although the way we measure our literacy has changed over the years. High as this rate of illiteracy was—and continues to be—several member countries of the OECD, including the United States and the United Kingdom, struggle with rates in excess of 20%. In 1999, barely half the adults of the world's least developed countries could read or write at all.

Yet Canadians are among the most educated people of the world. As of 2000, we spent an average of 11.6 years in school, an increase from 9 years in 1970. Only students in New Zealand, Norway and the United States spend more time in class, although only by a few months more than Canadian students. As of 1999, fully 89% of all adults in Canada had attended high school and more than 40% had graduated from university or college. Only Norway, the Netherlands and the United States had a larger proportion of people graduating from university.

Science and Technology

In 1874, the world's first light bulb was patented in Toronto by Henry Woodward and Matthew Evans; although unable to raise the financing for their invention, they sold the rights to Thomas Edison. In 1876, Alexander Graham Bell successfully tested the world's first telephone in a call from Brantford to Paris, Ontario. From those first two handsets, 98% of Canadian households now have a telephone.

Since the 19th century, Canadian science and technology have given the world inventions as diverse and valuable as radio broadcasting, the hydrofoil boat, the snowblower, insulin, and the Canadarm remote manipulator system for spacecraft. In 1995, a group of Canadian scientists developed a new type of banana—the *Mona Lisa*, which resists the many diseases and pests that have been threatening banana and plantain crops worldwide.

Canadians have also been breaking new ground in fog collecting—literally the practice of harvesting water from fog. In 1992, a group of Canadian scientists developed, for countries with little rainfall, a method that catches the droplets of moisture in passing fog and turns them into drinking water.

Canadians have been closely involved in the international effort to unravel the human genome—the blueprint for life contained within the DNA in each of our cells. Canadian scientists have developed several types of genetically modified mice for use in medical research. In 2000, a Canadian biotechnology firm successfully bred a herd of goats with a spider gene added to their DNA. The goats now produce spider silk, one of the strongest and most tensile substances on earth, in their milk.

"If no one in Canada knew our Anthem before the War, the Overseas men all know it now."

Ottawa Citizen, 1917

Worldly Ties

Canada has a long history as an active participant in multilateral and other trade agreements. Historically, we have had strong trading relationships in place with the United Kingdom, but with the start of the Second World War, our trading direction shifted south to the United States. In 1994, we were co-signatories to the North American Free Trade Agreement, and since then Canada's merchandise trade has grown by 80% with the United States and by a full 100% with Mexico.

The Empress of Ireland,

2000.

Work by Eric Walker.

Canada has also invested in developing markets; bilateral trade agreements are currently in place with Costa Rica, Chile and Israel while the United Kingdom, Europe and Japan continue to be important trading partners.

A generation ago, many Canadians were worried about the extent of foreign investment in Canada. Walter Gordon, a former Minister of Finance, could even refer to 'economic imperialism' in 1966.

Today, the tables have turned: Canadians are investing abroad at a much faster rate than foreign investors are investing in Canada. Between 1990 and 2000, our investments abroad more than tripled, involving mutual funds, pension plans and the expansion of Canadian-owned companies around the world.

In 2000, the United States continued to be Canada's largest foreign investor, although the Europeans succeeded in several large corporate takeovers. From 1980 to 2000, European investment in Canada came to some 20% of all foreign investment. Japan, Canada's third largest investor in 2000, owned $51 billion worth of Canadian stocks, bonds and assets—12% of all foreign investment in Canada. This contrasts with Canadian-owned assets in Japan of only $21 billion during the same year.

Tourism and Travel

"*Mont-Sainte Anne es una gran montaña*" explains a Mexican travel website, promoting one of several 'great mountains' in Canada where Mexicans come to ski. In fact, Mexican skiers and snowboarders have been hitting the Canadian slopes in record numbers. The ski market from Mexico, though still small, is growing quickly. In 1999, Mexicans made some 127,000 trips to Canada. Tropical sunshine also enticed almost one million Canadian tourists to Mexico and Cuba that year.

In fact, the World Tourism Organization ranked Canada as the seventh most popular tourism destination in 1999, when we welcomed 20 million overnight visitors.

Most of the tourists who visited Canada in 1999 were American. In 2001, American travellers made over 15 million overnight trips to Canada, spending over $10 billion travelling through Canada. Canada also attracts European visitors. The United Kingdom, Canada's largest overseas market, accounted for 780,000 travellers in 1999—more than ever before. French, German, Dutch and Italian tourists also flocked to Canada in increasing numbers in 1999, following two years of declining visits.

Many Asian tourists also visit Canada every year, especially from Japan and Hong Kong, although poor economic conditions in the late 1990s resulted in a decline in Asian visitors. Only tourism from Taiwan continued to grow steadily throughout the 1990s, so that Taiwan became Canada's fifth largest overseas market.

Nevertheless, as tourists, we continue to spend more outside our own country than international visitors spend in Canada. Since 1968, Canada has had a travel deficit with the rest of the world, though this has narrowed significantly in recent years. In 1992, Canadian tourists spent $6 billion more abroad than foreign tourists spent in Canada; by 2001, the difference was only $1.3 billion.

Whether it is to see the lights of Paris, visit the theatres of London or walk the sunny sands of Spain, Canadian travellers love Europe. In 1999, of the 10 main overseas destinations for Canadians, 6 were European.

On the other hand, fewer of us have travelled to other countries and fewer visitors have come to Canada, particularly since the terrorist attacks of September 11, 2001. The low Canadian dollar has also dampened our desire to travel abroad. However, following the attacks, the airline, aerospace and tourism sectors declined by as much as 18%. Largely, this was the result of a dramatic drop in the number of Americans wishing to travel, although by 2002, Americans were again on the go.

Certainly, the United States remains our number one destination. In 1999, some 14% of Canadians travelled to the United States at least once. Over two million Canadians

Untitled, 1997.

Work by Cathy Daley.

Photo by

Peter MacCallum.

visited New York State in 1999, but we spent the most nights (32.5 million) and the most money ($1.8 billion) in Florida, a popular winter destination.

The Environment

Canada, the second largest country in the world, has the longest coastline, the longest open border, and one of the largest supplies of fresh water in the world—almost one-tenth of the earth's supply.

As the keeper of so much of the world's undeveloped natural environment, Canada has joined in several international agreements to protect the atmosphere and land. In 1985, we ratified the Vienna Convention for the Protection of the Ozone Layer, followed by the Convention on Biological Diversity in Rio de Janeiro and the UN's Framework Convention on Climate Change in New York during 1992.

Mainly because of our cold winters, Canadians use a lot more electricity than people do in most other countries. In 1998, Canadians used an average 15,000 kilowatt-hours (kWh) per person each year, the electricity that a typical stove might use in 44 years. In higher-income OECD countries, the average was 8,400 kWh. Canadians are quite similar to the Scandinavians in this regard, but Norwegians consume considerably more: about 25,000 kWh per person or enough to run a small freezer for 100 years.

Some 62% of our electricity is generated by water. Although wind and solar energy produce some of the balance, most is generated through coal, oil, natural gas and nuclear power.

Foreign Affairs

Three days following the attacks of September 11, 2001, more than 100,000 people gathered quietly on Parliament Hill for a memorial service led by Governor

General Adrienne Clarkson and Prime Minister Jean Chrétien. "My heart," said one American, "is overwhelmed at the outpouring of Canadian compassion (for) Americans. How does a person say THANK YOU to a nation?"

Paul Celluci, American ambassador to Canada: "That day will also live in my memory as the day that I again learned the meaning of true friendship. That was the day Canada—its government and its people—collectively and spontaneously asked 'what can I do to help?'"

Such compassion and our further commitment to peace are fundamental to Canadian thinking and values. We are known as a nation of peacekeepers and are often called upon to play this role in international conflicts.

In 1945, Canada was a founding member of the UN, and several Canadians have played vital roles in the organization. In 1948, Canadian John Humphrey was the principal author of the *Universal Declaration of Human Rights*, and Lester Pearson helped to invent the modern concept of peacekeeping, for which he won the Nobel Peace Prize. More recently, Canadians have played a significant role in the creation of the International Criminal Court to prosecute those accused of genocide, war crimes, and crimes against humanity.

Since Confederation, in fact, Canada has maintained an active diplomatic presence in the world—at first, through immigration, trade and financial representatives overseas, and as of 1926, by representatives with full diplomatic status. (Vincent Massey, before becoming Governor General, was Canada's first appointment to Washington.)

The Department of External Affairs was established in 1909; countries within the British Empire and then the Commonwealth were not considered to be foreign. This explains why our representatives to Commonwealth countries are still called high commissioners, not ambassadors. In 1993, the department's name was changed to Department of Foreign Affairs and International Trade Canada.

"How can there be peace without people understanding each other, and how can this be, if they don't know each other?"

Lester B. Pearson,
Nobel Peace Prize, 1957

Poppy.

Illustration by

Neville Smith.

The Unknown Soldier "We do not know whose son he was. We do not know his name. We do not know if he was a MacPherson or a Chartrand. He could have been a Kaminski or a Swiftarrow. We do not know if he was a father himself. We do not know if his mother or wife received that telegram with the words 'Missing In Action' typed with electrifying clarity on the anonymous piece of paper. We do not know whether he had begun truly to live his life as a truck driver or a scientist, a miner or a teacher, a farmer or a student. We do not know where he came from."

—From the Eulogy for Canada's Unknown Soldier delivered by Her Excellency the Right Honourable Adrienne Clarkson, Governor General of Canada and Commander-in-Chief of the Canadian Forces, May 28, 2000.

In 1999, Canada was the seventh largest contributor to the UN budget, after the United States, Japan, Germany, France, the United Kingdom and Italy. Canada is also represented in the Commonwealth, the International Monetary Fund, the World Bank group of institutions, the North Atlantic Treaty Organization, the World Trade Organization, *La Francophonie*, the Organization of American States, the G8 and many other organizations.

With some 250 missions in about 180 countries and more than 800 trade experts around the world, Canada is central to a wide variety of international activities, both entrepreneurial and compassionate. From Leprosy Mission Canada to the Developing Countries Farm Radio Network, both in Toronto, there is also a strong and vibrant community of non-governmental organizations (NGOs) in Canada.

On another note, Canada is sending less money to help ailing countries around the world. In 1999, as a nation we gave US$1.7 billion, a 36% drop from 1990. What this comes to, for each of us, is US$55 through taxes (1999), and this is down from US$78 in 1990 and below the OECD average of US$66.

On Guard for Thee

On the afternoon of May 28, 2000, an unidentified soldier from a cemetery near Vimy Ridge was laid to rest in front of the National War Memorial in Ottawa. Canada's Tomb of the Unknown Soldier honours the more than 116,000 Canadians who have sacrificed their lives during conflict in the cause of peace and freedom.

An ocean away, in France, a stone figure stands on the top of the northeast ramparts of the Canadian memorial at Vimy Ridge, facing east and looking down at a single white tomb below. She is a young mother—a young nation—mourning her fallen sons.

Nearly 1.8 million Canadian men and women have served in wartime since Confederation—in the Nile Expedition (1884 to 1885), the South African War (1899 to 1902), the First World War (1914 to 1918), the Second World War (1939 to 1945), the Korean War (1950 to 1953) and the Gulf War (1990 to 1991).

In October 2001, Canadian soldiers were once again at the ready as troops were sent to Afghanistan in the international struggle against terrorism.

During the late 1980s and early 1990s, the collapse of the Soviet Union and the end of the Cold War significantly changed the Canadian armed forces. Canada cut military expenditures by 35% during the 1990s; by 1999, with 61,000 personnel, the Canadian military was 27% smaller than it had been in 1985 and represented only 1.3% of GDP.

Not three months after the September 11 attacks, the Canadian government announced $1.6 billion in new funding for the military as part of a $7.7 billion security funding package.

"Is it not almost a sin against nature, against hope, against happiness, not to look up at a flock of Canada geese as it passes?"

Dorothy Speak,
The Wife Tree, 2001

181

The Maple Leaf Forever In Bliss Carman's poem "The Grave-Tree," there's a stanza that runs: 'Let me have a scarlet maple/For the grave-tree at my head,/With the quiet sun behind it/In the years when I am dead.'

The maple tree and its distinctly shaped leaves have inspired poet, painter, musician and politician alike. One of Canada's several emblems (another is the beaver), it seems to have found a resonance in the Canadian soul as one of those rare symbols that unite us and even help us recognize ourselves.

In 1834, the first St. Jean Baptiste Society chose the maple leaf as its emblem and, in 1867, Alexander Muir composed "The Maple Leaf Forever," a song for Confederation and, as it turned out, one that would be belted out across the land by generations of schoolchildren to come.

In 1914, the maple leaf made its way to war, forming part of the badge of the Canadian Expeditionary Force, and troops used it as a stamp of Canadian identity during the Second World War. Not surprisingly, in 1965, when it came time for Canada to have a flag of its own, the maple leaf took centre stage.

Some three decades after Bliss Carman's death in 1929, a certain Alfred G. Bailey arranged for a maple tree to be planted at the poet's graveside. A quiet gesture, a requited request. A maple tree forever.

Maple Leaf.
Illustration by
Neville Smith.

(Page 184–185)
Killarney Lake,
Ontario.
Photo by Ron Erwin.

Credits and Permissions

Statistics Canada wishes to extend many thanks to the artists, authors and publishers whose contributions have added dimension and richness to this edition of *Canada: A Portrait*.

For literary excerpts, many thanks to the following: Sharon Butala (*The Perfection of the Morning: An Apprenticeship in Nature*, 1994), published by arperCollins*Publishers* Ltd.; Douglas Coupland (*Souvenir of Canada*, 2002), reprinted with permission of Douglas & McIntyre Ltd.; Roch Carrier (*Our Life with the Rocket*, 2001) and Stuart McLean (*Welcome Home*, 1992); both reprinted by permission of Penguin Books Canada Ltd.

Anne Carson (*The Beauty of the Husband*, 2001), used by permission of Alfred A. Knopf, a division of Random House, Inc.; Wayne Johnston (*The Colony of Unrequited Dreams*, 1998), reprinted by Vintage Canada in 1999 and reprinted by permission of Alfred A. Knopf Canada, a division of Random House of Canada Ltd.; Carol Shields (*The Stone Diaries*, 1993) and Dorothy Speak (*The Wife Tree*, 2001), both reprinted by permission of Random House Canada, a division of Random House of Canada Ltd.; and Margaret Sweatman (*When Alice Lay Down with Peter*, 2001), reprinted by permission of Alfred A. Knopf Canada, a division of Random House of Canada Ltd.

Roch Carrier (*The Hockey Sweater*, 1979), Lorna Crozier (*Inventing the Hawk*, 1992), the estate of Peter Gzowski (*The New Morningside Papers*, 1987), the estate of Margaret Laurence (*A Bird in the House*, 1970), Alistair MacLeod (*No Great Mischief*, 2001), the estate of W.O. Mitchell (*Who Has Seen the Wind*, 1947), and Michael Ondaatje (*In the Skin of a Lion*, 1987); all published by McClelland & Stewart Ltd. *The Canadian Publishers*.

The Minister of Public Works and Government Services and the Privy Council Office (*1996 Report of the Royal Commission on Aboriginal Peoples*), and Rideau Hall (*Eulogy for the Unknown Soldier*, Her Excellency the Right Honourable Adrienne Clarkson, Governor General of Canada, 2000).

For artwork, our thanks to the estate of Jean-Paul Riopelle, the Montreal Museum of Fine Arts, the Society for Reproduction Rights of Authors, Composers and Publishers in Canada (Sodrac) Inc., and Power Corporation of Canada, Montreal, for permission to reproduce a detail of *The Jacob Chatou*. The Canadian Museum of Contemporary Photography (CMCP) for *Five Generations* by Ted Grant, *First Communion* by Clara Gutsche and *Girl from Bathurst Inlet, Northwest Territories* by Richard Harrington. The Canada Post Corporation for permission to feature stamps from 1993 and 1995.

Bibliography: Selected Sources and Citations

The Land

Statistics Canada:
Annual Demographic Statistics,
Cat. No. 91-213-XPB
*A National Overview—Population and
Dwelling Counts (1996 Census of
Population),* Cat. No. 93-357-XPB

NRC. *The National Atlas of Canada
website:* atlas.gc.ca
Warkentin, John. *Canada: A Regional
Geography.* Scarborough, Ont.:
Prentice Hall, 1997.

The People

Statistics Canada:
*A Profile of the Canadian Population:
Where We Live (2001 Census:
Analysis Series),*
Cat. No. 96F0030XIE
Canadian Social Trends,
Cat. No. 11-008-XPE
Labour Force Information,
Cat. No. 71-001-PPB
*Census Profile for Canada
(1996 Census of Population),*
Cat. No. 95F0253XCB
Quarterly Demographic Statistics,
Cat. No. 91-002-XPB

Health Statistics at a Glance,
Cat. No. 82F0075XCB
*Dwelling Characteristics and
Household Equipment by Income
Quintile for Canada,*
Cat. No. 62F0042XDB

The Society

Statistics Canada:
Juristat, Cat. No. 85-002-XPE
Canadian Crime Statistics,
Cat. No. 85-205-XIE
Education Indicators in Canada,
PCEIP '99, Cat. No. 81-582-XPE
Education Quarterly Review,
Cat. No. 81-003-XPB
Health Reports, Cat. No. 82-003-XPE
*Statistical Report on the Health of
Canadians,* Cat. No. 82-570-XPE
Health Indicators, Cat. No. 82-221-XIE

Arts and Leisure

Statistics Canada:
Focus on Culture,
Cat. No. 87-004-XPB
*Canadian Culture in Perspective:
A Statistical Overview,*
Cat. No. 87-211-XPB

Bibliography: Selected Sources and Citations

Performing Arts,
Cat. No. 87F0003XPE
Sound Recording,
Cat. No. 87-202-XPB
The Canada Council for the Arts.
website: canadacouncil.ca

The Economy

Statistics Canada:
Canadian Economic Observer,
Cat. No. 11-010-XPB
Gross Domestic Product by Industry,
Cat. No. 15-512-XPB
The Consumer Price Index,
Cat. No. 62-001-XIB
Labour Force Update,
Cat. No. 71-005-XPB
Perspectives on Labour and Income,
Cat. No. 75-001-XPE
*Canada's International Investment
Position,* Cat. No. 67-202-XPB
*Canadian International Merchandise
Trade,* Cat. No. 65-001-XIB

Canada in the World

Statistics Canada:
*Canada's Balance of International
Payments,* Cat. No. 67-001-XPB

*Canada's Balance of International
Payments and International Investment
Position (Concepts, Sources, Methods
and Products),* Cat. No. 67-506-XPE
*Canada's International Investment
Position,* Cat. No. 67-202-XPB.
*Tourism Statistical Digest, 2001
Edition,* Cat. No. 87-403-XPE

OECD, *OECD in Figures, 2001
Edition.* Paris: OECD, 2001.
United Nations Development
Programme, *Human Development
Report 2001.* New York: Oxford
University Press, 2001.

Common Sources

Statistics Canada:
The Daily, Cat. No. 11-001-XIE
Canada Yearbook 1999 and *2001,*
Cat No. 11-402-XPE
Canada: A Portrait,
Cat. No. 11-403-XPE
*Historical Statistics of Canada—
Second Edition,* Cat. No. 11-516-XPE

*The 2000 Canadian Encyclopedia:
World Edition,* CD-ROM. Toronto:
McClelland & Stewart, 1999.

Regional Reference Centres

National inquiries line:
1 800 263-1136
Toll-free orders only line
(Canada and U.S):
1 800 267-6677
National toll-free fax order line:
1 877 287-4369
National telecommunications device
for the hearing impaired:
1 800 363-7629
Internet site: www.statcan.ca
E-mail: infostats@statcan.ca

Atlantic Region

Serving the provinces of Newfound-
land and Labrador, Nova Scotia,
Prince Edward Island and New
Brunswick

Advisory Services
1741 Brunswick Street
2nd Floor, Box 11
Halifax, Nova Scotia
B3J 3X8

Quebec Region

Serving Quebec and the Territory
of Nunavut

Advisory Services
200 René Lévesque Blvd. West
Guy Favreau Complex
4th Floor, East Tower,
Montréal, Quebec
H2Z 1X4

National Capital Region

Statistical Reference Centre
R.H. Coats Building Lobby
Holland Avenue
Ottawa, Ontario
K1A 0T6

Ontario Region

Advisory Services
Arthur Meighen Building
25 St. Clair Avenue East, 10th Floor
Toronto, Ontario
M4T 1M4

Regional Reference Centres

Prairie Region

Manitoba

Advisory Services
VIA Rail Building, Suite 200
123 Main Street
Winnipeg, Manitoba
R3C 4V9

Saskatchewan

Advisory Services
Park Plaza, Suite 440
2365 Albert Street
Regina, Saskatchewan
S4P 4K1

Alberta and Northwest Territories

Advisory Services
Pacific Plaza, Suite 900
10909 Jasper Avenue N.W.
Edmonton, Alberta
T5J 4J3

Pacific Region

Serving the province of British
Columbia and the Yukon Territory

Advisory Services
Library Square Tower
Suite 600–300 West Georgia Street
Vancouver, British Columbia
V6B 6C7

Index

Note: All references to Canada unless otherwise stated; "(i)" indicates a photograph or illustration.

CANADA

Scale: 1: 20 000 000

1 cm = 200 km

⊛ Federal capital

★ Provincial capital

● Other populated places

—·—·—·—·—· International boundary

—··—··—··—··— Provincial and territorial boundary

———🍁——— Trans-Canada Highway

Produced by Geography Division,

Statistics Canada